# We Are What We Are

Primal Songs Of Ethnicity, Gender & Identity

# We Are What We Are

Primal Songs Of Ethnicity, Gender & Identity

## Lopamudra Banerjee
## Priscilla Rice

Black Eagle Books
2022

Black Eagle Books
USA address:
7464 Wisdom Lane
Dublin, OH 43016

India address:
E/312, Trident Galaxy, Kalinga Nagar,
Bhubaneswar-751003, Odisha, India

E-mail: info@blackeaglebooks.org
Website: www.blackeaglebooks.org

First International Edition Published by
Black Eagle Books, 2022

**WE ARE WHAT WE ARE**
by **Lopamudra Banerjee** & **Priscilla Rice**

Cover Art : **Rhiti Chatterjee Bose**

Interior Design: Ezy's Publication

ISBN- 978-1-64560-291-0 (Paperback)
Library of Congress Control Number: 2022942137

Printed in the United States of America

# Preface

In this collaborative venture, *WE ARE WHAT WE ARE*, Lopamudra Banerjee and Priscilla Rice, both come across as feisty feminists, unabashedly unleashing their twin collaborative energies singing primal songs of ethnicity, gender, and identity which find expression in their powerful poems, essays, and monologues. Strongly influenced by Kamala Das, Sylvia Plath, Simone De Beauvoir, we find Lopamudra Banerjee singing her full-throated songs, her *'molten stories dying'*, and being reborn, gushing unhindered about the sordid darkness, vain lushness and the *'chaotic hunger of sweet- nothings'*.

Caught between two lands, one of her birth, and the other of adoption, her heart keeps going back to her homeland, Kolkata- to her childhood spent swinging from rusty swings, hopscotching, *'surreal festive songs'*, the smell of delectable culinary delights wafting from her mother's kitchen- smells mingling with the smells of alien shores, finally resulting in a slow, stoic acceptance of her present. Swirling in a miasmic loss, her city of birth continues to linger in her heart, like a soulful melody, soothing her frayed nerves.

The essence of her writings is encapsulated in the powerful words:

*'My life, the unraveled seed of a virgin poem*
*Let it be, let it be, Let it be clothed in fire unsheathed.'*
[*Unraveled*] and the nothingness *and the fullness of being'*
                                        [*Let me craft a poem*].


Priscilla Rice's words reveal a woman who loves life with intense fervor. Laced with a passionate tenderness, she talks about her grandparents and their snug home and all the farmworkers working there. In very poignant words, she writes about Santos Rodrigues, wondering about the dreams

and ambition of this twelve-year-old senselessly murdered on July 24, 1974, by Dallas police.
*"Did you catch frogs and horned toads in the backyard of your abuelo's porch and play streetball like so many of us did back then?"*
She asks, bringing a lump to the throat, and a prayer for all the kids lost to brutal violence.

In *Simply Be*, she echoes almost the same emotions as Lopamudra Banerjee when she says, I want to recognize all of my identities, [Mesquite tree from my childhood]
*'Today I ate some homemade bread [sent over by my tia Olga] that brought a tear to my eye'.* Recalling the childhood tree, which was *'the keeper of her adolescent secrets, swinging from tire swings, [in your silence you spoke to me]'*
In *Kay-So, a Manifesto*, she says with a fiery conviction, *'I cannot erase from where I come from.'*
*"I am not apologizing for my tongue and I'm going to let it do what it's gonna do'.*


Their nostalgic poems transported me to my childhood days and endless ramblings, hopscotching, tomfoolery, and slithering up and down the neem tree in my verdant garden. Through their combined spunky voices, they reiterate, that despite the rampant cacophony of the world, they will write and sing their own songs, dancing to their own beats, no matter what the world expects of them, and create a unique symphony. Both leave us with intermingled scents, sounds, secrets, silhouettes, and a well-spring of love for what was, what is, and what awaits in the shadows. Beautiful collaborative work.

*Dr. Santosh Bakaya*
*Internationally acclaimed writer of Ballad of Bapu is an academic, poet, essayist, novelist, biographer, Tedx Speaker, with more than twenty published books across different genres.*

# Contents

## Priscilla Rice

# Lopamudra Banerjee

*Poems, Essays, Monologues*

# Diaspora

*[Part of the combined poem by multiple poets/authors published in the special issue of Setu Bilingual International mag, 'Hyphenated Identities, August 2020]*

I let the rivers of my life run haywire, flirting with the uncertainty of miles that sprouted on summer nights.
I would come out in the open, unabashed, an earth unknown, cracking wide open at the edge of an unnamed surrender.
In that sacrosanct moment of a dark-throated song, the confluence of the east and west wrote its script of diaspora within my being like an irreconcilable truth, like the whisper of an omniscient God. Come, visit the rivers, the homes, the molten stories dying, and born anew, within me.

# Unraveled

To let every atom of a forbidden rain
Pierce my crust and core
To let the glistening pearls of sacred tears flow
when they gush, unhindered.
To bare open, surrender to the naked richness
of a flawed being
To embrace the architecture of flesh
and the poetry of a body
That has endured the lull of music
And the sordid dark of many a death.
To let go of the vain lushness of fairytales
And the chaotic hunger of sweet nothings.
To rest amid the fierce nudity
of many unborn verses.
My life, the unraveled seed
of a virgin poem.
Let it be, let it be,
Let it be clothed in fire, unsheathed.

# Hello Darkness, My Old Friend

*[A Personal Essay, first published online in Readomania.com]*

I was born only a couple of days back and resting in her arms. My dusky mother planted a soft kiss on my forehead the day she first met my baby skin – brown, drooling, eager to be one with her. Her offspring breathed close to her, a far cry away from the plastic perfection of fairness that was everywhere around her. She looked at me, a pre-term baby in skin and bones, at my chiseled nose and pouted lips. "You are beautiful, my baby girl, and you are just what I had imagined you to be", she whispered to me, while my tall, fair and handsome father roamed around us, held me sometimes, fragile and wailing.

*"Babar moton rong pelo na, Ma-er motoi kalo"* (She is not fair like her father, went after her mother). Voices hovered around her, hushed tones of human speech spilling over her kitchen chores, the mundane sameness of the days when she was busy watching over me, the sprinkling pearls of my baby teeth, the tapestry of my first uttered words. In the winged world of her dreams, I was snugly fit. She started painting it like a canvas, far away from the maddening voices that talked or cared about whiteness.

My mother's coral lips danced in love. Her tanned skin had been coyly wrapped in a bottle-green Benarasi sari the day she entered our ancestral house, following her wedding night. "The colour of your sari suits you, makes you look two shades fairer", women surrounding her giggled. My mother, with her brown skin, her bottle-green Benarasi, the raging river of her unsung songs, the sun of her presence, had been greeted that day into the house with the austerity of rituals, and the baggage of being the plain, charmless wife of a fair, charming husband.

Together, in our brown skins, we found ourselves, filling up with colors and scent, shadows and cool light, in the splattered splashes of Bengali vernacular music, of love, of poetry. Blackness had been our stained-glass window that sparkled and shined with our inner lights. As I was growing up, my mother would sew dresses for me in frills and laces, flowing frocks, skirts and *ghagras* in the most resplendent of colors. We never bothered to discuss skin tones. She never implored on me not to 'burn' my skin in the sun, to apply home-made fairness remedies or even fairness creams that grimaced at us from the TV screens, allured the ladies in every other household. Our lives were too full of her dreams about me, her incandescent light, brimming with home-made food and the everyday paraphernalia.

I grew up, comfortable, pure and true in the skin tone I inherited from my mother. Her brothers were dark-skinned, but whosoever bothered about the skin tone, or the physical beauty of men? Her only sister was light-skinned than her, and me, and our pictures together in family albums sang a delightful symphony of colors, shades and the various manifestations of all our genetic combinations.

In our science class, I learnt how melanin, a pigment that is controlled by at least six different genes, seeps into our skin, thereby playing an instrumental role in our skin colors. The two forms of melanin produced in our skins, pheomelanin and eumelanin, the numbers and sizes of the melanin particles and the bizarre biological details of their ratios, their queer, mind numbing permutations and combinations filled up my biology note-books. In my growing body, melanin held me tight, as it expanded and multiplied in the epidermis of my skin. I didn't know back then, and I do not know even today, whose genes it were that gave my mother her dark brown skin. It could be my grandparents, or even their predecessors. But I loved the dusk, the shadowy light that engulfed our beings when I hugged her, when darkness ran in our genes, solidifying our likeness, our bond even more. I began to love the overwhelming presence of melanin, the way it defined our textures, our bodies and our love.

….I clenched my fists, my teeth biting my lips and unspoken words as I paced up and down the stairs in a heavy, dark red Benarasi saree. *"Kemon gayer rong meyer* (How is the complexion of the girl)? … *"Ujjwol shyamborno"* (a brighter shade of dark), my mother had replied to the steady influx of queries of my mother-in-law, regarding my appearance. Darkness, that seemed an unacceptable stain in marriage alliances, was again, the color of Lord Krishna, the color of the fluted lover *Shyam*, which was perhaps made to sound soft, magical, to camouflage its unacceptability.

Under my brown skin, my soul glittered like an evening *raaga* on the night of my wedding reception, the soul that was pent up with silence and anguish as the ladies in my in-law's house irked at my skin tone. The make-up lady at the salon strived to whitewash me with layers of foundation and ivory face powder. *"Meyer gayer rong dekhe sari kenen ni* (Couldn't you choose a sari keeping in mind her complexion)?" She queried, nonchalantly.

I was seated in a chair, silenced, stoned. Between my ardent lips, straining to assert my love and the voice of unacceptability that failed to embrace me for who I was, something went dying that day. And in the days that followed.

A girl with dusky skin was obviously not on the list for

my mother-in-law, but her son had chosen me, in the days leading up to our courtship and marriage, celebrating the essence of both our unique identities. We had come together in the white light and poetry of love, a mutual admiration that originated from the uniqueness with which we both had written our profile descriptions in a matchmaking website. We trudged the road together on our own terms without parental interference, defying horoscope matching, defying all the primitive traditional trappings that would have defined our coming together. We both are dark, and white, in our own sweet little ways. With him, I string together the scattered pearls of my blackness and wear it like an adorning necklace.

Our two daughters glitter in the brown skin they have inherited from us both, their little bodies radiating with their own unique auras, while they are surrounded by Caucasian white skins everywhere, in the school, in our neighborhood, in their swimming and ballet classes, where I see them assimilating with the overwhelming whiteness all around. One summer day, while in her shower, my little girl of four asked me: "Mommy, my friend at school told me I have brown skin. Do I have light brown skin, or dark brown skin?"

In the pale yellow light of the bathroom, her tanned skin looked numinous and utterly loveable. "You have a beautiful skin, my baby!" I pecked her on her cheek, and added: "Doesn't matter if it is light brown or dark brown." I want her to take pride in and cherish her own skin, in the beauty of her own unique persona, and take the world in her stride, gleefully, victoriously.

# Thanks giving: A Requiem of Gratitude

*[Image courtesy: the poet, during one of her sojourns]*

On Thanks giving Day
I am thankful to life
For the mad swell of the familiar monsoon rain,
The mud of *Asharh-Shravan*,
clinging to my philandering skin still.
For the wintry mornings and the
Nicotine smell I remember of my father
And our mad bursts of bickering and
A silly wellspring of love that erupted,
we didn't know why, or how.
For the *surya namaskar* mantra and the *adya stotra*
that my mother would chant unfailingly each morning,
my eager eyes and ears, revealing themselves, by and by,
from the masks of innocence
Getting ready for the carnal, ruthless, world
where melodies and dreams still claimed their space.

For the wounds that slowly but surely turned to requiems
For the quiet deaths of many kisses, of many mangled
breaths,
Of many a sugar-coated love, hovering around
Like vain spirals of smoke.
For the closed doors of secrets that opened one by one,
Me signing a pact with each of them, smoldering in my
knowing,
muttering and then, shutting down, nonchalant.

For the girlhood lures and endless, endless ramblings
that turned to secret refuge with the passage of time.
For the journey of skin, flesh, blood and madness,
elusive dreams that could never be mine.
For the occasional cuddles and volatile cloudburst
that has made me a woman

For the journey of a nameless darkness,
My old friend and its deepest silence.
On Thanksgiving Day, I am thankful to God
Who made me an ebony moon, a lover
Ebbing into darkness, a starry-eyed mother,
Happily insane and fiery,
Writhing in thousand deaths and rebirths.


*Surya Namaskar:* Prayer to the Sun God according to Hindu scriptures.

*Asharh-Shravan*: Two months of the monsoon season in Bengal.

# We Are What We Are

Women.
Pathbreakers
Trailblazers and survivors
And purveyors, bursting
With perverse pleasure,
out to badmouth and belittle
one of their own kin.
Women, suckers of fairytales and gossiping
drooling on succulent,
recycled tales with no beginning, no closure,
Women, womb bearers and appeasers
Nurturers, torchbearers, witches and fairies,
Damsels in distress, victors and failures,
Sly and shy mistresses, wives,
Idolized and censured,
patronizing and bullying,
creating their own feminine wonders and paradise,
creating their own infernos,
burning in their own lackluster sameness,
drenched in their self-made puddles
of myths, inferences,
the tomfoolery of their beings.

# Let Me Craft A Poem

*[First published in Setu International Bilingual mag, 2018]*

*[Artwork: The poet]*

Today, let me craft a poem,
Not about my body
The rugged island of my throat,
The windy branches of my hands,
The dark winds,
The dispersed clouds of my wired bra
Today, let me craft a poem,
Not about the emitting flame of a girlhood
That had died in me, long back,
Watching silently over predators
Snapping at her,
And she, trying to snap back at them, became
Shards of broken glass
A cradle of unspoken truths
Ashes of stories about wolf-men.

Today, let me craft a poem,
Not about wilderness piercing
Through the woods of my body,
Cinnamon scent that hovers and swirls
Mouth to esophagus, cleavage to navel,
And beyond, shadows of lust
Lurking in civil obeisance, waiting to flow
In a deluge of primal wants.
Today, let me craft a poem, not about shades of scarlet
And the stifling silence
Crumpled, twisted into myths and high-flying tales
The tale of a virgin flower
The piousness of the flesh
The oft-worshipped rhythm of femaleness.

Today, let me craft a poem, an elegy,
a dirge of nakedness

Of both structure and content,
let me deconstruct, drop by drop
White-laced frocks and blooming springs
Barbie dolls and Cinderella's and erotic women
Twittering as temple sculptures.
Today, let me craft a poem on the nothingness
And the fullness of being
A pensive, barren woman,
An asexual, prose-driven woman,
An anemic, bulimic, *jihadi* woman.

# I Exist

*[First published in the anthology 'Ignite Poetry' (2020), edited by fellow poet/author Geethanjali Dilip.]*

The more you will talk behind my back
The more my fire will burn.
The more you will take me for granted
And write me off and crush my art and dissent
The stronger they will rear their heads
And resurface in their undaunted forms.

The more you force me to shed tears
And surrender my accursed, black moon,
pierce its crust and core in thousand pieces,
gaslighting and choking me,
The more i will come back, in ripples,
In torrential downpour, in brave, startling truths,
in an undying manifesto.
For truths cannot be slaughtered,
Art and dissent cannot wipe off from
The face of this earth, without burning,
Without flickering, without knocking you hard, for once,
without ripping off
Your own damned, infected pettiness.

For the truths that Maya, Sylvia, Simone, Jamaica,
*Kamala, Taslima, Mahasweta* have taught me unawares
Have instilled in me, will come out,
From the womb of my thoughts
From the web of my consciousness
And spill over, in spurts
Whether you throttle me

Refuse to hear me out
Pretend I do not exist
Write me down as a colossal waste.
I exist, a minuscule, shameless revolution
Floating in a tiny, raging bottle of wants.

*Kamala: Kamala Das, the very famous, spirited Indian author
and poet from Kerala*

*Taslima: Taslima Nasrin, the fiery, feisty woman poet and
novelist/memoirist from Bangladesh who had been exiled from
her own country for writing hard, indigestible truths about
women, patriarchy and religious fanaticism in Bangladesh.*

*Mahasweta: Mahasweta Debi, the famous feminist author
of Bengal, India with exemplary work on the 'adivasi' tribe
residing in the fringes of the state.*

# The Virgo Diary

*[In the month of September, generally known as the month celebrating the Virgo, or the embodiment of pure love that a woman stands for, my poetic tribute to the spirit of the quintessential woman, inspired by a painting created by the very talented artist, Kusumika Ganguly, my friend from Plano, Texas. While Kusumika's painting, as per my understanding, is a beautiful portrayal of tenderness, sensuality and the inexplicable divinity that is the essence of a woman, I have attempted to unravel the various mystic layers that reside within the sensuality of a woman.]*

In the month of Virgo, my endless sari
A work of *Meenakari* and intricate epic tales
Walks the wet, fertile earth, pervaded by her cosmic spirit.
I am completely immersed in my hills and crests,
My red, sensual vines which I cling to,
Blood trickling down, cheek to neck, bust to thighs—
A full-grown tree, a journey from womb to womb,
As I dance the spirit-dance, my cosmic consciousness
Waxing and waning with the sun's masculine rays.

I revel in my own sparkling redness, the red flowing
Like a ritual bathing of my moon flakes of self-love.
Dare speak about my blood-dyed hair, the contours of
A squashed fairytale as you brush past my shores!
In my trails of the earth, there have been little acts galore--
Little acts of coyness and creation, sex and the buried roots
Of a woman's innermost gnosis—moist, sweaty, gleaming.
A rustling of fleshy, succulent leaves, the milk and vagrant
rain
Of centuries of pent-up torrent, howling, raging, as I dance
The spirit-dance, my eyes shut in my divine unrest.

In the month of Virgo, my femaleness aches,
I free it from my moist breasts, from my deliriously happy
arms,
From my rivulets of tears. I let it roam, threadbare.
*"Yatra naryetsu pujyante ramante tatra devata…"*
They say: Gods rejoice within my pleats and folds,
I become the tender quiet of the beautifully stoic *Yogini*,
I become the pomegranate blood-drops of my majestic *Kundalini*.

Virgo is my second skin, the splinters and shards of the fetus
That bloomed into a babe, extracted from within me.
Virgo, my unborn progenies who would have reveled
In my crimson blood, flickering, blazing
In a world of Virgo folklores.

*Meenakari: intricate Asian/Indian design
*Yogini: the sacred feminine force/energy, Sanskrit term
for a female master practitioner of Yoga (sometimes
referred to as an incarnate of 'Parvati', the Goddess)
*Kundalini: Latent female energy, the kundalini energy
that resides in the esoteric body, a divine feminine force

# Otherness

*[Note: Written during a poetry and mental healing workshop in Washington DC, reflecting on the incredibly lone journey of a cancer patient.]*

My Otherness is the whiff of smoke
Settling in my wet, clumsy earth
A blurred mantra of smothered fairytales
When I comb chunks of hair falling,
With pale, restless hands,
I soak in the familiar smell of my Otherness.
My otherness, when I undress me,
Hangs loose, in the crevices of my moon flesh.
My Otherness settles in, like quick bursts of epileptic pain.
My Otherness, the solitude of the alchemy of my dreams
As they wash past my shores.
I am the night, the impenetrable darkness
The died-out candle of my Otherness.
Do you smell, sniff, taste my Otherness?
The burial ground of my peripheral being
Refusing to belong to the cacophonous oneness?
Like a moon's flickering rays
Just before her pivotal dissolving
I dissolve into the black sea
The dense, pirouetting dark of my Otherness.

# Raichak on the Ganges

*[Dedicated to my first sojourn at Raichak, West Bengal, India, just before the Covid pandemic compromised with my annual trips to India.]*

*[Image courtesy: the poet during her sojourn in Raichak, India]*

My poetry sometimes loses its moorings
In the cantankerous words of the urbane.

My poetry then, becomes a beautiful gift
Of 'shaluk' flowers nestled amid mossy ponds.

My poetry then, merges with the ethereal bounty
Of sunset by the Ganges,
When the pastoral green makes love with the old brick
fort,
When verses are written by the body of the river,
The flesh and soul of green meadows,
The rhapsody of an entire universe
built with the sweet nectar of Wanderlust.

My poetry sometimes ceases to be
Just a garland of words, images and snapshots.
My poetry then becomes one with the audacious scream,
The exclusive strength of Nature.

# Remembering Kolkata

The oily musk
The slashing downpour
The fluttering wings
And the clipped freedom
The drumbeats of my skin
The glittering Christmas lights
Park street, the embers of my thwarted wants
The smoke and soot-laden air
The tea-sellers of Maidan
The galaxy of friends
The myth, versus the reality
The choking familiarity and chaos
Of cab rides,
Of hospital rooms
Of the recycled ritual of death
The poetry of closures and catharsis
Poetry, that binds us all.

# My Mother's Kitchen

*[Inspired by the poem 'Indian Summer' by the Indian English poet Jayanta Mahapatra.*
*First published in Confluence, a literary e-newspaper from UK, 2022.]*

Chanting and waiting
The mornings of cardamom tea,
'The Mouth of India opens'.

The intense swirl of the 'daal'
Cinnamon courses through the curry's veins,
Spoonful of offerings, splintered flowers.

Grandma's last wishes, the subterfuge of loneliness.
The wrinkles, the loose ends of a melody
Tattooed in the cumin-favored bits.

Mustard seeds float over warm water,
I return to my familiar coconuts and moist air,
I return to rough summers, the Norwester winds.

Milk, sugar, bay leaves, mumblings of ancestors,
"Don't touch!" The rice pudding, still boiling hot!
I return to slippery floors and mother's kitchen smoke.

Heated aroma, scurrying past somber wind,
Long afternoons, dreaming of the concoction
The unexhausted story of Indian spices.

*Daal: The Indian version of lentils cooked in a broth. Here I refer*
*to the Bengali 'daal' which is lentils cooked in a savory curry.*

# Kumortuli

*[First published in Setu, the international bilingual mag and later featured in Stanford University's special project 'Life in Quarantine', their digital humanities archive.]*


The *karigar* opens the lock gates of the body
Of a Goddess he has almost formed,
He lets me dab the brush with watered clay,
And I find my fingers swaying the brush
In the traffic intersections of the bosom,
The rib-cage, the dainty neck and the loins.
"You're a mother, aren't you?" The *kaarigar* says.
"Take my brush, the Mother Goddess I am making
will be complete with your touch…"
I look hither and thither, take the brush
Try to invoke the sleepy troughs and crests of a figurine
That would soon enliven in some corner of the world
Exported as a Goddess with a name,
a special *tithi* to ritualize her presence.

In the nondescript alley, faces hide and come out,
jeering, loquacious, quiet, intimidating, bodies
With half-fed stomachs, runny noses,
pronounced rib cages, lack-luster hair.
Faces of infants latching on to their mothers' emaciated
breasts,
Faces of impatient sentinels, men, women and their
offspring
guarding mossy, crippled structures, brittle roofs
And stairs leading to the scum and openness of drenched
streets.

Their homes, privy to many a starving night canopied with fragile sleep
and dense nonchalance. We roam around the precincts,
My over-enthused buddies and myself, our poetry, our cameras
and flashes, our clumsy fluttering mismatched with their primal wants.

In the glum streets, the heavy-breasted *Durga*, the poised *Saraswati*,
the indolent *Shiva* and the feisty, nude *Kali*, the pensive *Shakuntala*
become the flashes of lightning, the welcoming droplets of rain.
In between our urbane banter, the *karigar* and his almost formed
clay-Goddess, craving to be enlivened
The fullness of a ritual, a flickering, sensual truth,
A holy semblance of life sustained, holding on to its tattered edges.

*Kumortuli*: A community in North Kolkata, in the east region of India where artisans craft idols mainly of the various Hindu Gods and Goddesses and also make statues
*Karigar*: Artisan
*Tithi*: A special date to worship a God/Goddess according to Hindu rituals
*Durga, Saraswati, Shiva, Kali*: Hindu Gods/Goddesses
*Shakuntala*: The wife of King Dushyant and mother of Bharat, a female character in the epic Mahabharata

# A River Within Me

*[First published in the anthology 'Reverse the Rivers, edited by fellow poet/author Geethanjali Dilip.]*

A river within me knows all my high tides and low tides,
The sun's birth, descending on my banks and the sundown
Melting my fiery skin into dark forebodings
Of death, and rebirth.
A river within me knows my light, motion of time
And my fallen moon at night, the hungry, volatile dance
As I spin around my moist, sacred space, like a child
Spinning inside the womb, waiting to be born.
A river within me is the smell of my elemental lust
As I become the ruthless watcher, my bank made soft
With tears of throbbing life, of funeral pyres.

With the river within me, where do I go?
Converge with the sea of garrulous memories, shrink or
grow?
Take in all the fish coming up for air, all red embers
That turn to grey ashes? The river gushes right in,
Settles within, slowly, with its waning moonlight,
Its eager darkness,
Its placid body, its secret, superfluous chatter,
Its keen onlookers.
The river scampers, smells inside me, I lose myself
In its body like daily offerings of poetry and surreal passages.
A river within me fills up and swells, and I become
Its wind and melody, its continuum flow,
like birth, death and rebirth.

# The Scarlet Rain

*[Dedicated to every girl attaining womanhood, and to her rocky journey in attaining it, a journey where she is bound in chains, a journey where she discovers her absolution.]*

(1)

When I was a little over nine, I smelled flower in my bath.
Every night, my dreams rained, the flowers swept along.
My dreams were pieces of cut glass, odors entered
And withered away, the night hung in my mouth
Stale, unwashed, bleeding away.
Unzipped, squatting on the bathroom floor
The blood washed the night from my flesh,
Then swirled around the wet tiles like shimmering fish.
My mother and aunt supplied cloths, tied
Napkins in tight strings as blood gushed inside me,
Hammering words in my ears, insisting I should be happy
To grow up, surrender to this monthly leaking.
They called it by strange, funny names,
Tickling laughter, making it a reminder,
A lovely, shy inheritance.
I smelled flesh every time I ate fruit,
In my tongue, I tasted the stench of chopped, peeled skin.
When I was a little over nine, I walked dainty,
Fairy-like, my smiles spreading with sparkles
And songs. I bled and smelled slaughtered animals,
And rain. I saw in colors, beautiful ones,
The dark unknowing, the swelling of seeds, buds, flowers.
The year revolved around spotty clothes, fumbling,
The bumps and holes of hormonal wavering.

(2)

When I was a little over nine, and bled for the first time,
I didn't know my lips, the sweet swelling of curves.
I didn't know how bodies floated, shivered in caress
I didn't know how girls were slapped, blindfolded and
raped.
I didn't know the voyeurism of men.

(3)

My body has weathered the cycle and calendar
Of bleeding, birthing, milking. My body is a moving train
With a pout, a cleavage, and legs that spread
In between cycles. My body stops at the edge of surrender
Resting against yours. Feel my heart breathing a love
poem,
Or coax my flesh into yours. Know my blood, tears and
sweat,
Or veil my face within locked bars. I bleed the scarlet rain
Of generations—surging, writhing, crackling, moaning,
Boiling like stew, melting away.

# Grandmother Mine

*[For my grandmother who was the first one to call me a feminist
when I was only thirteen. First published in The Kali Project
anthology, Indie Blue Press, 2021]*

Grandmother mine,
I am the legacy of your progeny,
The flesh and bones of your seed, your flesh,
The slow death of your sounds,
drenched in threatened subservience.
I wake, roam around your ancient seas
Birth life, rattle loud, screaming against
Supremacist songs.

This is how I survive—
Cooing your Bengali rain songs,
Building my cocoon around overdose of memories
Your horror stories of leaving behind
The torn, shaken Bangladesh.
The river *Padma*,
Mothering my girlhood revolution.

I am the forbidden dance,
The onset of new seasons
The distant language
The thirst and the rhythm
Of a revolution
which you had learnt well to deny.

Grandmother mine,
I am the déjà vu of your centuries of stories
The unborn cadence of your language

You had wrapped with crushing silence.
I am the importunate one, inhaling hot oil
In your airless room where you sometimes spoke
Of matriarchs and feminists-to-be,
Of nomads whom your cracked earth
Could no longer sustain, or shelter.

I wake, between continents
The skin of my ancestors planted in my embryo.
I am the renewed song of your thirst,
The hunger of my mother,
Dressed up in a liberation song.

This is how I survive—
Chopping and screwing old definitions
Of the womb, making claims on my body,
Writing down its verses in blood and dark ink.

# Indianness: The Metaphor of the Misfit

My Indianness is the bookmark
of sweaty summer musk,
Tucked within the creases
of a self-same, overused book
In the slice of space where
memories of *rickshaw*-rides
And an old *ghaat* lay suspended
in a remembered patch of air.

My Indianness is the honks of buses,
yellow cabs and the odd stir
And jerky moves of local trains
 and subways in a jetlagged return
To another home, responding
to a speck of reason.
The froth of my *bangla* catch-phrases,
in unwarranted, white-infested places.

My Indianness is the shameless squirt of inabilities
Which makes me an oddity
in a land where new sojourns
are embarked on, new road turns are made,
with pronounced insolence.
My Indianness is my scorching inferno,
as I shuttle between safe-same chores.

My Indianness is my white wallet
purchased from the dollar store
The chain of it that opens up

to reveal two pockets,
One carrying dollars in five, ten,
the other, rupee notes saved
From auto-rickshaw rides, a fleeting whiff
of homes and hearths, abandoned.

My Indianness is the everyday injury
which I can't bury always, safely.
The fervent flicker of memories,
the occasional dents in the brain
unfazed by changing colors,
the blinding maze of lanes, by-lanes, highways
When all around me, the sweet lure of amnesia
wins over others so easily.

My Indianness taunts me
as I dream of houses moved in, in my slumber
Houses with cement stairs
and the sparks of tube-light,
and crickets chirping
Outside large glass windows
covered with white blinds.
As I hang on a thin rope,
flanked by odorless comforts and dusky sorrows.

I write verses, stories on diaspora,
my Indianness, a nameless brook
That craves to be one with a mighty river,
a vain promise to dilute
Thick foams of whiplashes,
onslaughts, residues of soot.
My Indianness is the perpetual rebellion,
the telltale signs of embracing mess.

*Ghaat*: River-bank

*Rickshaw*: A vehicle used in India and some other Asian countries, a light, hooded vehicle resembling a three-wheeled bicycle, sometimes hand-pulled, having a seat for passengers behind the driver.

*Bangla*: Bengali, the Indic language spoken in Kolkata (India) and other parts of northeastern India and Bangladesh.

# Buddha

[Gautama Buddha, the primary figure in Buddhism, the enlightened teacher, monk, sage, philosopher lived and taught mostly in the northeastern part of ancient India sometime between the 6th and 4th centuries BC (Before Christ). The painting and poem have been inspired by the *Lotus Sutra*, his meditative teaching originally in Sanskrit, aiming to enable individuals with deep insight about life, wisdom and salvation.]

My Lotus love coagulates,
The Buddha in me waxes and wanes.
I breathe in the silk
and blue of seven births,

The water, pregnant sighs
of old, reincarnated flood,
The flood trails along tolerant soil.
The green of youth,
the unblemished flesh of the earth,
my ancestral musk.
My lotus love coagulates.
Buddha, the milk of love
The liquid ocean of soundless dreams
That I smear in my cracked earth.

My lotus love is the bleeding poetry of centuries
The unacknowledged fragrance and light as I slip
Through the cracks of an earth,
Erupting in edgy, volatile loathing
While I carry my own human stench,
Caressing a slow-poisoned tomorrow.
The Buddha in me is the sudden surge
Of quaint syllables and chanting learnt
In the fading twilight of a friend's company.
My lotus love coagulates in the acrylic touches
Of a painter's delight, and parables relived
Amid the dark daily venom. Bodhisattwa, Buddha,
The unfailing ritual of soul,
The ebbing, flowing continuum of hope.

# The Divine Calling

I am a makeshift believer, nestled in the bistro of this life.
In my kingdom of faith, the Divine emerges, sometimes,
As the throbs in the azure sky, as the cloudburst
Dancing in spirals, breaking free in torrential rain.
Sometimes, amid the twinkling lights in the pulses
of a traffic, huddled close, with sweat and convulsive bursts.
Sometimes, as pebbles thrown in placid water-bodies
Causing rebellious ripples, sometimes, in the eyes of
Nomadic globetrotters and carefree toddlers
I happen to cross paths with, in airports,
in shielded supermarkets, in nondescript cafes.
Sometimes, the Divine emerges in the prancing and preening
Of a woman in love, walking down the alleys,
Waiting for her Krishna with the flute.
Sometimes, the Divine pirouettes as the image
of a ravishing *Devdasi* dancing with her entire cosmos,
prostrate at the feet of a stoned God,
A high-priest, eager to usurp her.
Sometimes, as the image of a grand temple
with mythical, legendary sculptures
The feminine anatomy, a testimony to my own body
Which can be a temple, a mosque, a church, or a *gurdwara*,
A religious zone where I might allow some to enter,
In curls and twirls, welcoming my jagged edges,
my hungry rain songs.

In my kingdom of faith, the Divine emerges, sometimes
As the *raaga Iman, kalyan, behaag,* gliding up and down
my undomesticated veins,
As I pull myself to perform a holy chanting.

In my kingdom of faith, the ethereal Goddess Saraswati
and her *veena*
Dances in the membranes of my haywire brain
along with the neurotic pleasures of gobbling up banned
books
where humanity thrives, indolent, shameless.
In my kingdom of faith, *Durga, Kali, Chandi* dance the
spirit dance
of creation, and apocalypse, the witches and fairies reverse
roles,
Kings in epics become demons of misogyny, demons in
myths
Become neglected, half-told truths.
What do I do, when in my kingdom of faith,
The cascading terrains of the sacrosanct and the
sacrilegious
crave to play, wreak havoc, gush out in rhythmic waves.
I am a makeshift believer, nestled in the bistro of this life.
In my kingdom of faith, the Divine emerges as scattered
blotches
of long-nurtured anonymity.
The Divine emerges as a long, unnamed poem
Shedding off its bulky cloak of religion,
I kiss its unbound beauty
And it takes me in, my crust and my core.

*"Tomarei koriyachhi jeebonero dhrubatara/E Somudre aro kobhu*
*Hobo na ko dishara/Tomarei koriyachhi jeebonero dhrubatara."*
("O Divine, I have made you the brightest star of my sky,
the anchor
Of my sojourn into the sea of this life. With you around,
Let me not turn astray, anyhow, anywhere.")
A voice sings within me, deep, unfathomable,

The voice Of a dead bard, whose songs, lyrics
Turn into a secret offbeat rhythm
Breathing inside an amusing, roaring inner world
Where trees swaying in the heaving wind,
Girlhood tales of river bodies,
The light and darkness of endless mornings and nights
Turn into scriptures, pious utterances, pilgrimages,
Turn into the holy incense of surrendering.


*Lines from a song composed by Bengal's Nobel laureate
Rabindranath Tagore, which is part of 'Gitabitan'*

# Sita's Open Letter To Her Twin Sons' Wives

*[An imaginary letter written by Sita, the tragic heroine of the Indian Hindu epic 'Ramayana' to her daughters-in-law, wives of her twin sons Luv and Kush, long after she chooses to perish in the core of the Mother Earth which was her origin, according to the epic. Sita, Lord Rama's wife, was kidnapped by Ravana, a mighty demon king of Sri Lanka during her stay with her husband in a jungle as an exile. Later, after killing Ravana in an epic war, when her husband Lord Rama brought her back to his kingdom, he ordered for an 'agnipariksha' (fire-test) for her to prove her chastity. In essence, the long poem is a dramatic monologue in the form of poetry which is a vehement protest against the patriarchal construct which is the basic premise of the epic 'Ramayana', according to my understanding.
First published in the anthology 'Mytho-Manthan' (2017)]*

From the earth's hidden core, my home, there I rise.
The salt of my ebony kohl dragging me,
Surreptitiously, to yet another grim story, one, I am afraid,
Might be the awakening of yet another epic, a descent into
Images and memories that I fight still, the bliss of shadows
You all love to call a 'myth'.
For you, my daughters-in-law, married today
To my twin sons 'Luv Kush', the two chunks of my heart whom
I had bathed in my anguish, nursed with my milk and blood,
Put to sleep in a bed of rocks in *Rishi Valmiki's Ashram*,
In the piercing pangs of my exile, are being married to
yet another perfunctory, pitiless song.
Today, in the HOLY shrine of *Ayodhya*, the shameful

embers
of the fire of my sanctity test still smolder with a
rambunctious smile,
The glaciers of a vain king's valor and his exemplary act
of banishing his wife never melts.
The haughty, insolent ten heads of *Raavana* burn
amid the festivities of the *Dusshera*, the fallen king
who had claimed me once,
whom my valorous husband had slain in shards.
Tonight, in the cradles of the self-same dynasty,
Your acquiescent selves take in the garlands, the vows,
The womanly rituals that bind you in holy matrimony to
my twin sons,
I lurk in a quiet nook, an abandoned cranny of the
illustrious palace,
My long dead, cold contours cracking open the earth's crust
Which had been my self-chosen exile, the umbilical cord
I had spitefully returned to.

The epic had sealed my fate, I know,
For I had been more of a pawn than of a woman,
My simmering, perfumed tale of marriage, obeisance,
abduction,
exile, motherhood and sanctity, constructed,
deconstructed.
The King, my lord and his Kinsmen, buzzing like bees
around him
had nipped my sanctity in the bud.
Ah yes, 'Sanctity', the word!
It had become a stale, festering wound, a bruise
That the confusing clamor then had failed to see.
Today, unbeknownst to your dreamy, virgin eyes,
I look on, forlorn, lost, as the marriage pyre coughs up

the blood and phlegm of that very promise of 'sanctity',
the allegiance, the bows and vows, steady, insistent, yet
irrelevant,
and I stare, eerily, at the crimson of *sindoor* in your head-
partings,
The floodgates to yet another ravishing epic of deception.

I have learned to unlearn the salt and pepper
Of my smudged, chaste femininity. My twin sons,
Carved in the mirror image of the revered Rama, my lord,
All set to unleash yet another fiery tale of 'Fortitude',
A hard-earned name at the cost of betrayal, humiliation.
But for once, you, my daughters I had never borne,
Breathe in the Sulphur of my trails,
Before being sucked into this rancid epic tale.

# Sad Songs Are Born in the Kitchen

*[First published in 'Voices Within', the anthology of Setu publications, 2021]*

Monochrome songs
Bloated aftermath of honeyed tea.
You know the long, wet hand
The fingers of a strange, drizzling sky.

The sky, overcast with jabbing words.
The black-and-white fool's dream
Scream of the earth
Inside sad songs
Vaporized longings
Formative lessons
Missing pieces of puzzles
Born in the kitchen, piercing the void
Between half-cooked broth and bruised fingers.

You know there's no real hero in the portraits
Hung on the walls, and you burnt your own, looking
away.
You know you are neither the mistress or the muse,
Only the body of a woman,
Only an ounce of ignited fire and the blood drops of a
spirit wild.
You know the summers on porches and the mad swell
Of rain in your throat, tingling with verses.

# Green

My grief is green with the scum of stories.
I wish it would rise from the buoyant dark of my neck
Like old, unfiltered bile,
Spread across my trails
like liquid tales of desperation.
But like a steady, insistent rhythm,
It stays on in my zillion caustic breaths,
The green settles in my poison-friendly throat
And I sink, in daily dribbles, in the rubble of my chores.

The green, they say, is the color of melancholy.
Unanimously, they contend and I know
My skin peels itself, loosening over the edge.
My melancholy stream dances within my rims and crests.

I am a mountain of cracked earth and raging silence
Overlooking a green river where unseen fungi
Of a warrior woman stretch across continents.

# A Memoir Springs Out Of Nowhere

*[First published in The Quiver Review, June 2021]*

(1)
Faltering, stumbling
Unlettered years
The promise of a runny fish curry
The promise of a *puja* with rituals learnt
With stale flowers refreshed
Unexpected Decembers
In search of a home where reunions never happen
anymore.
A memoir springs out of nowhere.
Starting in the damp courtyard where it was all a child's
play--
Worshipping the false Gods, rhythmic reminders in
shrines,
Learning about primal yearnings
And the smell of burning incense,
Shaking the dust from truant feet.

(2)
A memoir springs out of nowhere--
From the storm churning in the nomad mind,
From the deceased mother's recipes of *shaak bhaja*
And the reminders of brewing it all well,
The ripples of salt and the landscape of Bengali tongue,
The yin and yang of teapots and pressure cooker.
A memoir springs out of nowhere—
From the body where the first clods of red earth appeared

To the body that rained, frosted and then thawed again,
between continents.
From the sweaty hands, losing control over
the verdant staircases of girlhood,
and the alien steering wheels.

(3)
The scent of New York, Texas, Nebraska, Kansas,
Florida, California, Arkansas
The colors and strokes of four walls, of makeshift hotel
stays.
Metamorphosis of storms and crisp skies
breaking up into home, shelter, refuge.
A memoir springs out of nowhere—
From the urgency of kilometers
to the stoic acceptance of miles,
From the night shifts in between transits
to the smudged settling in adopted homes.

*Shaak Bhaja:* A Bengali delicacy of spinach stir-fried with
eggplants and Indian spices.

# Frida: A Journey, An Anthem

[Note: First published in 'Voices Within', the anthology of Setu publication, 2021, this particular poem, a dedication to the feisty, volatile Mexican painter Frida Kahlo and her paintings has been inspired by an astoundingly beautiful photograph of Kahlo, (1943), courtesy Guillermo Monroy. I have tried to paint a portrait of the beautiful Frida while looking into the photograph.
Source: Frida Kahlo Postcards]

*[Artwork- sketch of Frida Kahlo: by the poet]*

Head dresses and womanly fetishes
Stark portraits of transitions,
Passion, often renamed as hedonistic art.
Frida, do you know how often
you give generations of women

bleeding with rhythm,
beauty and banal reminders
The dreams of dangling ear-rings
and ravaged red hearts
displayed with pride?
Bruises, like shimmering flags
fluttering around bare
work-in-progress body parts
wafting like slain poems,
when we can say
we don't even give a damn
if we are ever marginalized,
or trivialized, or whitewashed,
or given the license
of trickling tears
after each blow, each coercion?
Flecks of stardust around our shedding skins,
fingers shriveling, aching to craft miracles
with the subterranean flow of naked, stifling truths.
Stroke after stroke, each part of us
gagging and loosening, leaking, abandoned.
Rivulets form. Ripples form, merge,
magic strokes our skin, we sing primal songs.

# Sisterhood: How Our Stories Merge

*[The inspiration for this poem came from a special issue of National Geographic magazine and its cover image. In the issue, the cover story was on two twin sisters of mixed parentage, a seething commentary on race and biological identities. The poem was first published in the anthology 'Equiverse: A Sound Home In Words', September 2018.]*

Stripping the tautness of our skins
Flesh, bones, marrows, the algorithms of DNA
The hunger in the bits of our souls,
Roaring, raving till the shores, where we find ourselves
Bare, unlit, maddening, sisters whose stories merge.

For eons, we swam in the scum of our ancient memories.
The lightness of my skin, the ebony song of your
blackness,
The inheritance of my ruthless blonde hair shutting me in,
The legacy of your thick, lustrous brownish black mane,
Sprouting like a manifesto of liberation, dying to break
free.

For eons, we have arrived, our bodies smelling
Of unabashed placenta, running over the zigzag course
Of our races, for the world had forgotten
How you and me, both are streaks of randomness
Emerging from the wanton lust of the universe.

Come, let us merge, collide, our stories,
The thunder and rain, the turbulent skies of generations.

Let me wipe away your coagulated bruises
As you take me in, to absorb my weary lineage of
whiteness.
We become twins, scaffolded in our freedom, our
yearning, our lingering sameness.

# On The Earth Day

*[Written on the Earth Day, 2016, in memory of a street child
I saw in India some years back. First published in the online
edition of 'The Dawn Beyond Waste']*

You have seen my absurd chuckles
My coos and gurgles as I revolved
In your orbit, sunk in
My mother's emaciated breasts.
Did you revolve with me, Mother Earth,
While the starlight gazed at
Flowery, full-endowed children?
While the full moon welcomed them
With the whiffs of her spices?
Did your night sky melt when, at three,
My nimble fingers devoured by my parched mouth
Craved to count your bountiful stars,
My hungry body, resting in the littered city streets?
When I dreamt about floating in your placid shrine,
My eyes opened up to dry patches of dirt?
At seven or eight, I have peeked through
The plastered walls of schools where the blue globe,
staring at me like the harvest moon
Summoned me, the kohl-lined eyes
Of the teacher tracing its curves,
I never knew the Equator; the Mediterranean
never ebbed and flowed
In my scarred, burnt-out days.

But even I knew how
The last drops of monsoon smelt,
its juices ricocheting off my pockmarked face.

I am the earthen salt of the grimy, molten streets
they trample every day.
At sixteen, even my frothy foam shimmers,
dances in zigzag sunlight.
At the call of twilight, when mud and filth
pops out of your blades of grass,
I paint you, Mother Earth;
Craft you with the folds of my stained palms.

The cosmos around, a commotion of rebuffing times.
Are you rattling, Mother earth, staring at me, tossed aside
As I clutch at your slithered pieces? Do you, for once,
Look at my papery wrists,
think you could have nourished me better?
See how my torrents still sing your songs,
See how our jagged edges shine
as I drown within your crevices,
Threadbare, spiraling in my earthen wants.

# A Poet's Plea

*[Written for the Tata Steel Literary Meet #kalaam 2020, Kolkata, India]*

In the proverbial City of Joy,
As I seek harmony amid the din and clatter of disparate
sounds,
The foggy late winter sky carries tales
Of every street corner, every *Azaan* and prayer,
Many a human birth, many cremations, many burials.

I, a deconstructed poet, writhe and burn.
A massive, deafening noise of disdain picks
Out of nowhere, in my land which,
I all along knew
Was accustomed to bridging gaps between creaky doors,
Bridging continents with the bubbling mindscape of
poems and stories.

Where do I find myself in this miasma of loss?
In my mind, my city dwells
In the confluence of the river Ganga and the oceans,
In the fluttering wings of my fellow artists
Chiming in unison, our verses casting motions of feathery
flights.

All of us—hungry, lost, yet illuminating.
In my mind, let my city linger softly
A soulful melody of Oneness
Amid disparaging metaphors of Change.

# Sun Temple, Konark

*[Image courtesy: The poet, from her sojourn, January 2020]*

When the rocks and the divine sculptures
Engraved in them breathe poetry,
Do you need the aid of verses in concocted words?
When divinity spells its untainted songs
In a mosaic of figurines,
Quaint and mighty in the same breath,
Do you need the Gita, the Bible, the holy Quran?
When *Prakriti* and *Purusha,* the elemental man and woman
Converge in a volcanic ocean of wants,
Do you need any other melody,
A divine rhapsody of some other form,
More voluptuous, eroding your senses,
Your faith in all-encompassing love?

Konark, am I your courageous, piercing need,
Your bursting sunshine, the wrenching pain
Of centuries when you evolved?
Am I the spurious birth of a dream
In the palm of your hands
As the world breaks open
In a thwarted call for a revolution?
Am I the evening prayer of the woman in her high tide,
Or the bitter, twisted lies that she wraps
Around her to feed parochial urges?
I keep my bejeweled tears,
The depth of my bosom,
The womb of my history
At your feet, and leave you for now.
Let me come back to you again in another lifetime,
Years older and starving.
Let me come back as revolutions keep brewing,
As you wax and wane, explode fiercely,
Wrenching out smiles,
Your unclipped verses of freedom.

# The Courtesan Loved A Man

*[Dedicated to the courtesans who lived in the heart of Lucknow, India, where young girls were sold off to the 'kotha', forced to live their lives inside that establishment for the rest of their lives, and pined for lovers whom they could never marry and claim as their own. The poem was first published in the anthology 'Equiverse: A Sound Home In Words', September 2018]*

Do not speak ill of my frost-bitten love
For years, me, the fallen *tawaaif*, have unleashed
My art, my ravaged moon drops, my intoxicating
loveliness
On you, my anklets, my bangles, my head-dress
Crackling like untamed fire, bursting open, petal blooms
of rain.
You have been drunk on me, poured your putrid breath,
Your directionless lust on my *sringaar*, and yet,
I have never been betrothed to your sweet-toothed love!

Go, find your chaste woman waiting to fling herself
In your promiscuous arms, warming up her womb
For yet another of your legitimate male heirs,
While I remain your coquettish mistress of the camp,
Struck by the insane Cupid's darts, in much the same way
As that foolish zenana of the inner quarters of your home
Where you step in and step out like sudden shafts of
lightning,
Drunk, inflamed, your every command,
Your blazing trails, her entire earth
That you suck full throttle, yet take pride
On being the all-consuming man.

But then, remember, my potent man,
We both are toying with our tumult, salt rubbed
On hidden wounds, while she feeds you her aromatic *pulaao*,
Her bashful looks, mapping each of your turns, your bends
Which she hopes to navigate, even if for a single night,
And while I, the insolent fire, keep burning all night
With my wanton dance, a hot, sensual downpour
Waiting to ensnare you, yet again, the next night,
I still trace the contours of my hometown, far away
From this forbidden feast of spring, my childhood
Of sugarcane and paddy fields, the lassi my *Amma* made
That I had right on the day I was blindfolded, my mouth
gagged
In the paddy field, deflowered by men of my own kin
Then sold off, bleeding, writhing, banished
From the elixir of my little nook at home and the open
courtyard.
It is all there, when I close my eyes,
Resting my flames in your inviting chest, or waxing and waning
In the overused bed, shedding torrents of bitter tears, all alone.


Do not speak ill of my frost-bitten love
It has traversed the length and breadth of many hills and
slopes
Bumps and ridges, desert dunes and the endless tunnels
Of my womanhood that you have chased,
Looking for a million signals while I have suffered
The sacrilege of being the *tawaaif*, the public woman.
In the forlorn *kotha* nestled in the fringes
Of the city of the royal *nawaabs*, my heady beauty
Wafting in the arid air like jasmine bloom
Has long lost its virginity in your sloppy kisses,
Your papered notes, the dense forest of your bare chest

Soon after I had learnt my *gayaki* of the melodies,
The peacock dance that made you come to me,
Like a moth towards the flame.
Shabnam, Mehek, Noor, Laila, my inmates
We grew from young buds to the lotus courtesans
Embracing the muck around us, as you come
And claim us all, bit by bit, our bleeding rains
Falling incessant, fractious, unyielding.

# Once, After a Torrent: Prose-poem

*[Artwork/sketch: the poet]*

My love, once you had gone so far as to love the fire
within me. I did not think then, some day you would burn
away the fiery bird, running to and fro within
my neatly feminine voice, your sensual fuel.

Once, my love, you had colored me in wild hues, the red
of my heart,
The blue of my veins, the green of my fertile womb.
Have you ever known, how I too have craved to lick, suck
away the red, crisp edges of your heart?

How I would barge into your home, that primal nook of yours and become your bubbled-up Venus?

I, that unacknowledged *Dalit* girl who might have emerged like a nameless egg from the pits of the cracked earth, I, who have lived so much in your lustful eyes that the mirror has showed me your hunger a zillion time. I, who have loved you with such vigor that I run away from you, ingesting your kicks and blows, and then, come back like that ghostly phone call you get after a tiresome, earth-shattering torrent. Didn't I ever tell you I would come back at my own will, from Burma to Bangladesh, from Sri Lanka to the crowning glory of the Taj, being the sandbar, my subterranean flow, drowning the sanctioned peripheries of your home?

Wait, do you seek the embers of yet another fallen love in my smudged vermilion, Did you sense ruins in my crimson lips?

My love, once you had gone so far as to eclipse yourself in my dense, dark undone. My love, once you had vowed to leave everything behind, live penniless in the crooked streets, sheltered only by the moonbeams tucked under my cheap, crinkled sari. As I look into your eyes today, just after that earth-shattering torrent, it's not the whiplashes of that self-deprecating love, not the juvenile teardrops of the tyrant memories, not the fierce bleeding rose of my tender eighteen.

I seek the primal fire, the scandalous crescendo and fall in my blood and veins, a charred anthem of an unborn revolution.

# The Unforgiving Rain

*[Written in tercets, my small poetic tribute to women who dared
to dream, no matter what their ancestral histories have taught
them.]*


Thump, thump, thump,
The colicky dreams rise, unforgiving
Burst open against the swallowing silence of nihilism.

Instantaneous, uncowering
In heat, dust and sweat, the drumbeats go on
As they dance on the edge, avalanches of unforgiving blasphemy.

The unforgiving rain
The sister storms in the wooded trails
Know their mettle. They've stayed in place for thousand years.

Forgiveness is saintly.
But only the unforgiving queens know that to be humane,
They would wriggle themselves into the arms of an
unapologetic thunder.

Smelling of blood
And a wasteland of stories of forebearers forgiving every grain
of perpetual sin, they unleash the unforgiving showers
and the world gives in.

# For Simone De Beauvoir

*[A reaction after reading parts of 'The Second Sex' by Simone De Beauvoir, French writer, intellectual philosopher, political activist, feminist, and reflecting on her words as a woman from the Indian subcontinent.*
*First published in 'The Kali Project' anthology.]*

The last time I woke up,
I remember, I demanded a third space.
A space that meandered
from the hopscotch square
Of estrogen games, from the erectile brain
of testosterone urges.
A space of my own desperation of belongings
'The Second Sex', a requirement of my syllabus,
An elusive continent, a vociferous sea,
A torrid landscape of my own making.

Simone, I hadn't known your name
The feel of that fiercely unwomanly woman
When in my girlhood, cascading beauty
of princesses and heroines spilled
all over our barren courtyard,
from the basket of my grandmother's tales.
Love was the promise of a sanctioned cacophony
of children to be birthed, the language of coercion
As kings banished queens for sons not born,
Princes' lip-locked with princesses,
'Hail thee, patriarchy!'

The last time you twisted and turned us
In our dreams and sold us a ticket to witness

The vestiges of war between our own troubled selves,
I remember, we had pushed some boundaries,
But there were some barbed wires
which were better left on their own.

The last time your words entered my realm,
"One is not born, but becomes a woman,"
I remember the dark hunger, the denial,
The act of letting go, the truth of our beings.
Simone, we, the 'other sex', reborn, recycled
A zillion times, have been churned, fermented
Reclaiming our spaces in the fickle humanity.

# Instruction Manual: How To Be That Badass Woman Poet

*[First published in the anthology 'Witness: The Red River Anthology of Dissent', 2021]*


How to turn to a badass poet
From a domestic goddess is easy.
Just unlearn your cuteness for the essential dark,
Stay on in the pitch-park galaxy,
Marinated in sacrosanct words.
Play on in the tumultuous sea of sounds,
Metaphors, diction of old poets
Take a line from here, a whiplash of pain from there,
A jingle, a whisper and a surreptitious peak
From the flammable past.
And then, in your own sticky canvas,
Shed them off, along with
Your engaged arms, your heaving breasts,
Your womb and birth canal,
Replace them all, the sexist jargons you learnt,
And lucid memories of labor
With your nascent, blood-soaked poetry.

Then, after you knead the dough
Of fickle human stories,
Divide the dough into little sacred mounds of word-flesh,
Born from your ancestral womb
Into the cradle of feminine fantasies.
And then, slowly, crisply deep fry them
With tenderness and affliction,

Fry them some more like children birthed
Post the gestation period,
As you try to make a home
Out of the vestiges of war within you,
The rubble of the overgrown cities within you,
Born between your immigrant dreams,
your becoming, your unbecoming.

To become a badass poet, to be reborn
A hundred times is as easy as it can get.
Only speak to the unfamiliar earth
With your unbridled wet body every time you see
A smoke of an unborn poem, a triggered survival act.
Only speak to your displaced self in the language
Of desperate desires, your tattered earth and sky.

# Radha's Refrain

*[Written during Holi, the festival of colors as I reflect on
the tragic plight of Radha, Lord Krishna's paramour after
Krishna left Vrindavan. Lord Krishna happens to be one of the
incarnations of Vishnu in Hindu mythology and a principal
character in the Hindu epic Mahabharata. The poem, written
in the melancholic voice of Radha, in a Roseate Sonnet
form inspired by Dr. AV Koshy, also represents the tragic,
monochromatic lives of the widows who live their lives in the
fringes of Benaras, the holy city of India, worshiping Lord
Krishna, as their 'Shyam'.First published in 'Reviews', an online
literary journal.]*

*Shyam*, my heart bleeds the red of your scars,
This Holi, let me pour on you my frothy pain.
Let the rain bleed blue, dissolving my black moon.
Let me burst forth in charcoal rain.
*Shyam*, this Holi, let me not hide the tickling taste of black.
My moon is a Death Valley, calling you back.
*Shyam*, this Holi, let the monochrome moon be our muse.
Let this Holi be a war poem, us splashing around, fragile,
loose.
My roof is tilted, sagging in a world of murky colors.
I grope in the empty dark, my skin reeks of unknown
odors.
'*Raaslila*', the sun-kissed gold of your '*sringaar*' evades me.
Oh, my coarse lips parch, unable to sing that song, lovelorn.
Sing to me, let us be ruffled, threadbare again.
Effervescent, let us catch the black moon
and sleep in its boughs, forlorn.

Raaslila: The legendary *Raas* dance that Lord Krishna danced with his paramour Radha and her *Sakhis* (female accomplices) in the idyllic Vrindavan, according to Hindu scriptures including *Bhagavat Purana*.

Sringaar: One of the nine '*rasas*', or flavors/emotions, usually related to romantic or erotic love, attraction or beauty.

# Kalbaishakhi

[*Artwork: the poet*]

My *Kalbaishakhi* whirlwind, I beseech you.
Shake me, ruffle my being in the pitch dark,
Your dense clouds roar and rave,
I lose my vain ornaments, my catastrophic pride.
Let it be, let it all pass...
I am dying to be one with your moist bosom,
Your heady aroma, I am dying to copulate,
Squeeze tight, hold on to your bare, brazen truth.

This *Kalbaishakhi* whirlwind, my Radha meets her Krishna
In the tide of teardrops, in a tempestuous night
The *abhisara*, the union of dense, surrendering souls.
The orchard of youth melts in a restless, orgasmic
downpour.
"*Asharasya prathama divasa*", the first luscious, breezy day
in *Asharh*, the monsoon month,
The torrent opens boundless doors.

My Krishna's flute, blowing in the haywire wind
I unmask in amorous ripples,
I become the wellspring of love of the feminine energy of
Ganga,
Who unfolds her lush beauty, her opulence
Only to her pensive, precious Santanu.
My lovelorn soul immerses in the elemental burst
of '*Viraha*', the blues of separation, as the river banks flood.
My sudden verdant splash, an untimely refrain,
I return to the water and torrent, my primal force.
My *Kalbaishakhi* whirlwind, I beseech you,
Unlock my virgin wonders.
I am the '*Prakriti*', the irresistible flower of nature.
Let me merge with my '*Purusha*', my magnificent Man,
Let us bear fruit in the mad gust of this night,
In this wet, wild awakening.

# Wanderings

A pale, dusky afternoon
Has stored all her hysteric sobs
And the dusk of a river Ganga
Settling itself like a young girl
Getting a hang of her newly worn sari,
Arranging the pleats.

In yet another part of the world,
Distant, but in the same hemisphere
The boats drift away from one another,
And find themselves river-less, anchor-less,
Counting on the submissive waves
in the middle of nowhere.

Somewhere, in the nameless, moist paddy fields
A juvenile pair of feet trample over a wrong bed of crops.
The morning sun had fallen over an open courtyard
Round, succulent like the full-grown navel orange.
And like a jolt flanking her, she remembered the ones
Who had wiped away the dewdrops of her girlhood days.
The divergent roads leading to the wide stretch
of grassy patches blow away into shreds,
And she feels she is no more in the earth's grassland.

The sky is a constellation of nameless fields
And pale, dusky afternoons of dust, soot
and a speck of memory
The dusk of the river Ganga, her lonesome trails
Around the earth's orbit.

# Fire and Storms

*[First published in the anthology 'Earth Fire Water Wind' in 2021]*

I hope the fire that has smoldered within me
Before the beginning of my scribbles and dialects will
flicker again.
I hope the onomatopoeia of the poetry of this world,
Crouched in the dark, hopping and skipping
Towards a yet unseen light will find its moorings again,
Bouquet in one hand, and in the other, the weapon of wisdom.

I hope in yet another land, languishing and sighing,
Primordial storms churning in my mind,
I reconcile with tastes, smells, sights ever changing,
As my smudged kohl stops
Stinging with impossible yearnings, brewing over time.
I hope in skin, bones and blood,
I absorb the collected ashes and songs of grief,
Dressing myself in layers of the earth, metamorphosed.

I so hope, in circles of longing, we will rise,
In our burnt-out truths, in the carvings of a new world.

# Love Poem For America

I call you a crystal-clear fluid
Coursing through my veins,
Sometimes, you give me walls to shut me in,
And let me slide into devouring linens
And smells of shadowy rooms, the ebb and flow of sex.
I have drunk you whole, your silent fumes
And labels, your grocery stores and undusted streets--
The way I have drunk my morning coffee,
But our childhood is unshared.

You, for instance can never meet
My six-year-old self, swinging in a rusty swing
Running over hopscotch squares in the open terrace
And see the bouts of my father's temper, the rituals of cigarette
Burning in our old verandah, footsteps swirling in the house,
The first rains that bore flowers hanging from the boughs,
The widowed aunt making the dough of delectable *pati-sapta*
For the *Sankranti*, and the surreal festive songs.

In the remembered wind drift, our presents collide,
And I stop, seasoned, ambivalent in your tracks,
Watching the cars blur into the swift obeisance of traffic,
The vernacular poetry that had exploded into the mouth.
I hang loose, somewhere between acknowledgment
And the steady, insistent odor of change.
I can never meet your splintered history of assimilation
Your postmodern lies, the curse and blessings of alien tongues,
Your spirit of ambition and your self-portrait of a day's bruises,
Sadism and broken homes, your camouflaged mirth.

Here, I lap up your shores, back in my space
Between washed skins and heaps of laundry, and write
A love poem for you, remembering my suburban skin
And my ancestral ashes, the dusky rivers traipsing in
between.

# Last Wish

*[Dumdum airport, Kolkata, Winter 2018]*

Linger in my body and soul
Like the moist air which I've inhaled
as my mother's body metamorphosed into an urn of ashes.
Linger in my body and soul
Being that warm, ardent kiss of my first lover,
Linger in the fresh, iron smell of my blood-red lips
as he sucks the virgin blood from my lips.

Linger in me, being my infant want
for my mother's milk which I never had,
Linger in me, wafting like the enigma of friendship
between elusive light and darkness.
I will seek you, tethered to the reminiscences of my lost days,
Days which have dissolved in the crooks and bends of
unnamed alleys.

Linger in me, like the thousand thwarted revolutions
wrapped around my being,
Which never found their closures.
Linger in me, like the sticky oil ruining the pillow on the bed,
And crinkled noses complain, how fishy, how obnoxious
the bed smells.

Linger in my body and senses, being a rhapsody of my desires
After making love with my beau,
Linger in my soul, as the quintessential Pragya-Parama-Prakriti,
The clarion call of childhood pals.
Linger in me from one birth to the other,

Victoria, Shahid Minar, College Street,
The dingy lanes of the Hedua of my youth.

Come to me when I turn into a corpse,
Come and touch me with your magic wand
As the flames of my pyre burn.

# Read Me:

### A *prose-poem or monologue*

Do you desire to read me, sitting on my boughs, my bark, my branches, stubbornly, tenaciously clinging to me? Do you desire to read my verses, lyrics of my angel choirs? Well then, read me at your will, construct and deconstruct my lissome letters, words, fragments, ravaging them, wreaking havoc on them, penetrating their volatile contours. In this night garden of your throbbing wants, cut open my roots—violet, indigo, red, magenta and fire, and leave the imprints of your bleeding lips. Cut open my roots as you spread your wrath and venom on me, curse me with your hissing prose and brisk rhyme, but still, read me. Read my crimson tales, my perforated core, grant me immortality as you still read me.

Read me whole, read my light and intense parts, read me as you find me ugly and lopsided and crazy and magnificent all at once, read my discarded heaps of scraps even as in your conscience, you crave to wash down, unlearn the lessons of my body. At the end of it all, why do I see you then, prostrate at my feet, your lofty head drooped at the edge of my arms in inevitable surrender?

What did you see in the quiet, subterranean flow of my gestating words? Did you read it all, and become a fallen human, like me? Well, no, trees are felled, women are rendered fallen, maimed, but men, the rest of humanity stay static and true, true to the volumes of history and myths written on the landscapes of time, true to your flesh, bone, blood and soul. Read me, still, dark and barbarian at one end and opaque, marble-white at the other end. Read me till the end of time, till the apocalypse of the sexes lets you construct and deconstruct me in lust, passion, anger, domination, subservience. Read me, till there is nothing left to collapse, to incubate, to germinate.

# Patriarchy and the Female Gender: As I have Seen It

*[First published in the website of The Red Elephant Foundation spearheaded by Kirthi Jayakumar, under their 'Intersectional Musings'.]*

*"Each time a woman stands up for herself without knowing it, possibly without claiming it, she stands up for all women."*

Maya Angelou

As a little girl fighting with the demons of an early puberty in the late 1980's, my first tryst with my own intimate world shaped by the patriarchal construct happened one fine August day like a rude jolt, shaking me from my girlhood reveries.

"Your elder cousin sister, in her college, had been quite a rebellious one, you see. She used to mingle with many boys of all religions and castes and of all backgrounds, quite indiscriminately. One summer evening, quite a decade ago, she had been to the cinema with this unruly herd of friends, and the news reached her father as quickly as a wildfire."

As much as I remember now, it was close to my twelfth birthday, and there was a school project that required us to make an elaborate family tree, an initiation that would lead to revelations and pride in chronicling one's roots. As that uninitiated twelve-year-old, the onus was on me to understand, rather internalize the Bhattacharya family tree, the quirks, preferences, socio-cultural identity of my ancestors. However, the first aspect that struck me in that journey was the cultural conditioning of the women in our family. Much later in life, I learnt to spell and know the full significance of the word 'patriarchy.'

"And then, he got so furious with her the moment she returned home, he threw at her the aluminum bucket with which he was having his evening bath."

"Oh dear! Wasn't she hurt? How did she deal with it?"

"She was hurt, yes. In fact she has that scar till today, a reminder of how her father, your elder uncle would be instigated to react once she dared to cross her boundary line."

Yes, the boundary line was etched out for me too, in this memory of woman to girl conversation, one of the many random number of chit-chats that happened between me and my mother in our suburban home in West Bengal. In her conversations in which she shared little anecdotes on her in-law's family, our ancestral home in the same suburban town, I would hear, time and again, the sound of a door opening up bit by bit in front of my maiden eyes, leading to various nuanced understandings of gender roles, gender discrimination, and the choices that women in my familial periphery would or would not make, not without their repercussions.

After more than two decades of this revelation, resting my body and conscience in a foreign soil, I have tried to decode the legacy of my family, noting down its bare particulars.

A middle-class Bengali Brahmin household, with a stern reputation for being casteist, cornering women in the name of well-nourished, unexplained family traditions. Inter-caste marriage of a daughter could lead to being ostracized for years altogether, only to be reunited with the family after a male offspring had been borne. Inter-religion marriage was inconceivable, and if it happened, it would only result in banishment. Widows, both young and old would absolutely have to live a life of rituals and celibacy, be on a strictly vegetarian diet and remain within closed doors during any auspicious family occasion.

Exhibiting religious allegiance to the minutest details of the Hindu faith, including fasting, reading scriptures, reciting mantras et al. "Don't forget the rich legacy of us Brahmins, your grandfather has been a priest and a Sanskrit scholar for years." I had been reminded at every turn.

Has the female gender been oppressed in such households? I don't think they seriously gave it a thought. They were sent to schools, colleges like any other, allowed to practice extra-curricular activities (as long as their in-laws have no issues with those post-marriage), some of them have been allowed to continue their jobs after marriage. But the boundary line was clear. The sexual expressions had to be minimalist, they had to be strictly conformist to the ideas of race, caste, gender and religion. Otherwise, they would be in dark waters, and they happily surrendered.

Nobody in my family has been exposed to Maya Angelou, Simone De Beauvoir or anyone who have raised thoughts about female sexuality, liberation and dissent. Reading the banned books of the exiled writer Taslima Nasrin has been a sacrilege that I have indulged in proudly for over twenty years now. Had not my persona been shaped by the discovery of their books, art and poetry, I wonder I would have been only one of them, steeped in the shackles of their tradition, never knowing the boundless universe and its creative energies.

# Priscilla Rice:

*Poems, Monologues, Essays*

# Two Worlds. Dos Mundos.

*[An essay from a southwest Texas Tejana]*

When I'm asked where I'm from, I always say "Texas" or
"Southwest Texas." Both are true.
But when they ask me three times: "But where are you
really from?" And I play dumb as if I'm not understanding
the question as I repeatedly say "Texas, Texas, Texas."
Eventually, they give up or end up asking what they're
really asking, which is: "What country are you from?"
Well, Texas is in the U.S., so I'm from the U.S.
Eventually they walk away or think I'm rude. How dare
I not reveal my ethnic identity and family history when
asked! I've learned a way to deter those who absolutely
HAVE to know.  I mean, God forbid, a girl with a brown
face could actually be from here and from many places.
But this is home.

 I identify as a multi-ethnic Mexican American woman.
One of my great grandfathers crossed the Rio Grande
during the Mexican Revolution, some came on a boat via
the Atlantic, and some were already here. I honor all of
my ancestors. Because of their persistence and audacity to
exist, I exist.

I never was asked that question "where I was from" until I
left Crystal City. It's frustrating to feel like you're not from
here or not from there – especially when your ancestors
are from many places. I have called myself Chicana,
Latina, Mestiza, Latinx, Tejana, and many things.  I'm all
of those things. I carry my Mexican culture in every part of

my being. It's the culture I most identify with, growing up in close proximity to the border.

As a child, I would cross the Piedras Negras, Coahuila, Mexico/Eagle Pass Texas border with my family to see the dentist or to go shopping or to have dinner at El Moderno, a fancy restaurant with a pianist and waiters who wore suits – a luxury that didn't exist where I was from. In retrospect, it truly was a privilege. As a kid, I didn't realize that. Despite my physical appearance, I knew the moment I spoke, people would know I was a "gringa" or from the "other side". I wanted to belong. I wanted to belong in Mexico and here. I've struggled with acceptance in both places. I don't blame my Mexican brothers and sisters. I would be distrustful too. I mean, who do I think I am?

It's unfathomable to me how people can live in Texas, a state that overwhelmingly has Latinx people (from here and all over the world), and yet they consider us a monolithic group. In fact, we have many identities and have origins in many countries. I almost cried when my DNA test revealed that my lineage is linked to 14 different counties. Identity as a person, as a woman, as an artist, as someone who is constantly interrupted by men (mainly white men) is something I fight for daily. I want to break the mold of all the identities that people have imposed upon me. I want to recognize all of my identities and simply be.

Being fetishized when exes or potential lovers have asked me to speak to them in Spanish (even if they didn't speak the language) or being told that I speak English so well has been the reality of most of my adult life. From the ages of 18-48, I've dealt with this frustration.

Identity is complex. It's something I continue to discover, even when I'm constantly told who or what I am as a Latinx, as a woman of color. Embracing all of my identities, especially the homegirl from southwest Texas who says hello and will give you the benefit of the doubt until you show her you are NOT "buena gente." These pieces are an exploration of the heart and soul of this Crystal City/Dallas woman who loves life with fervor and passion – acknowledging my past, my present, and where I'm going. Adelante.

# Majestic Mesquite de mi infancia
## (Mesquite Tree from my childhood)

In my state of semi-consciousness
waking up from turkey and tequila dreams
Today I ate some homemade bread (sent over by my tia
Olga) that brought a tear to my eye
And I visited the old mesquite tree de mi infancia, from
my childhood
Big little boy Cristiano climbed the majestic mesquite tree
in grandma P's yard
The one who let us swing on tire swings
And provided us shade to play in
Protecting us from the hard Southwest Texas sun
That kissed my beautiful Morena skin
We kids Playing "canicas"
and making a plan about how many games we could play
before the sun went down
How many horseshoe games with grandpa L were played
under the old mesquite tree?
Or cuántos barbeques did grandpa make en un pit –
making his signature B-B-Q pollo
I can still picture the smoke reaching up to the highest
point of the tree
*Majestic mezquite, ¿qué me dirás? Dices que mi amor no será capaz*
*De dejarte nunca nunca nunca*
*Jamás te dejaré, jamás me dejaras*
*Tus brazos y tu cariño son dejarás*
It you look closely at the top of the tree, its branches and
leaves look like a corazón,
As an amiga was quick to point out
Grandma P says that tree was there before the house even
existed,

the house that belonged to great grandpa Marcelo
This is my family's sacred ground
Tierra sagrada
Where dreams were planted …..gardens of bougainvilleas
and tomates y zanahoria y chiles
 …all types of chiles
The ventaja of coming from farmers
Who knew and worked the land
Mom says she remembers climbing you as a little girl,
with my tias and tio
She's sure you're at least 100 years old, but old mesquite, I
know you're older
They say that mesquite trees can live up to 200 years
Or more
Qué cosas hayas visto, dear mesquite?
You're so inviting old mesquite
You love kids so much
Always waiting with open arms
Con los brazos abiertos
Inviting us to be close with you in your branches
You are like our great great great great grandmother
How many times did I climb on you and just
contemplated life
And you gave me so many answers
In your silence, you spoke to me.
I always thought that when your leaves rustled in the
Southwest Texas wind
And the dirt smelled like tierra mojada
(boy, do I love the smell of wet dirt right before a big rain!)
You spoke with me
"Don't listen to that boy" you said
Or "follow your dreams" you said,
 "no les hagas caso"

"You can do it, mija"
"Don't worry. You'll leave, but you'll always come back,"
you said
And I have
Through divorce and two kids – both boys
*Majestic mezquite, ¿qué me dirás? Dices que mi amor no será capaz*
*de dejarte  nunca nunca nunca*
*Jamás te dejaré, jamás me dejarás*
*Tus brazos y tu cariño son mi paz*
You have stayed the same
And I, the eternal tree hugger
Always go sit by you or go up to hug you
Even as the arrugas invade my skin and my cintura
changes sizes
You are the same, old majestic mesquite
The keeper of my adolescent secretos and childhood
dreams
You were once a pirate ship or carried an invisible tree
house
Or once we were the lost boys who never got old
Because you are eternal
You will outlive us all, old mesquite
Promise me when I'm no longer here, that my sons can
come visit you
That they can hug you and you will keep their dreams and
secrets too
And give them hope
Because things may change, but you will always be there
Throughout the generations
You will always be home.
*Y si no regreso,*
To my boys, you will be home.

*Majestic mezquite, ¿qué me dirás? Dices que mi amor no será*
*capaz*
*de dejarte nunca nunca nunca*
*Jamás te dejaré, jamás me dejaras*
*Tus brazos y tu cariño son mi paz*

# Betabel

*[Este poema es un homenaje para mis abuelos Petra y Luis y*
*todos los trabajadores del campo, que nos alimentan día a día*
This poem is a tribute to my grandparents Petra and Luis
and all of the farm workers, who feed us day to day.]

1960s. Carrizo Springs, Texas
Last day of School
*Ese mismo día que se acababa la escuela*
On the very last day of school, *mi abuelo le decía a sus hijos:*
*"arreglan sus cosas porque vamos pa'* Minnesota"
*Y mi abuela y sus hijas* spent the evening packing
Packing clothes, packing shoes, packing sartenes, etc etc
Preparing for the next few months spent away from home
So the very next day Ramos family of six left in la
madrugada to Minnesota y North Dakota
*Para trabajar en el betabel*
*Grandpa compró a trailer o como dice grandma "un trailito"*
*Y ponían todas las cosas para hacer la comida, clothes, y todo*
*El viaje a Minnesota y North Dakota*
*Horas y horas en el carro*
*My mom, tías y tío cansados*
*Entreteniéndose en el viaje*
Inventing games along the way
*Después del viaje*
La pizca de Sugar beets, betabel
From sunrise to late afternoon
6am on the road to the field/
*pa'l campo porque estaba retirado de donde se estaban quedando*
*Era puro trabajar, mija*
It was nothing but work
Tractors on site

*A cortar hierba del betabel*
*Limpiarlo,* clean it
*Hasta la tarde*
*Trabajo de 6am hasta 6pm*
*Trabajando para alimentarnos*
*A pesar del trabajo duro, fue bonito dice mi abuela*
*" porque Conocimos North Dakota y Minnesota"*
The only other places she had traveled to outside of
Carrizo Springs and
Her hometown of Cienega de Flores, Nuevo Leon Mexico
*Y el fin de semana cuando ya tenia unas 3 semanas de trabajar*
Grandpa would talk to the *el jefe y les daba dinero por el*
*trabajo que hicieron*
*Iban al pueblo a comprar*
They'd drive to town to buy clothes
*Las tiendas ponían todo bien barato - -*zapatos, blue jeans,
And grandpa would tell his daughters *"Logralo, vayan."*
And my mom y sus hermanas y su hermano would buy clothes
*We'll see cuanto alcanzamos para comprarle ropa a los*
*muchachos, decía mi abuelo*
When it was time to go back home to Carrizo,
*Allá venían muy contentos mis hijos,* grandma said
*con sus tennis shoes*
*Iban bien vestiditos,* well dressed with new shoes and blue jeans
*Bien contentas mis tías y mi mama*
Grandpa Petra and Grandpa Luis would say to their children
*"Necesitan seguir con sus estudios para que tengan una*
*educación, para que no trabajen así"*
You need to continue your studies so you can have an
education, so you don't have to work like this
Grandpa shared those same words with me, his
granddaughter, *muchos años después*
*Estudia mija, me decía*

Grandma (my only living grandparent) says that grandpa
was very poor growing up
*Eran tan pobres*
Losing his mother at an early age
Being the oldest son,
And having to leave school at 6th grade
To work to support his siblings
*Pero si tenia talento tu abuelito*, dijo grandma
*Era buen trabajador y buen hombre*
Thank you, grandpa, for passing on your wisdom
Thank you for feeding my soul
For sharing your plantita knowledge
Nourishing me and helping me grow
Thank you for working and honoring the land
To everyone like my grandparents
Who gave their life and continues to give their lives to feed us
Who nurtured us with food, stories, and consejos
Who have worked the land
And continue to work the land
*Un trabajo digno*
*Que merece mucho respeto*
I see you, I hear you
This is part of my family's story
*Trabajando en el betabel*
But there are many stories
right now
Families working in the fields to feed our nation
*Familias trabajando para alimentar nuestra nación*
From sunrise to sun down
You honor and respect the land
And we must do the same
By honoring and respecting you

# Kay-so, *a manifesto*

I can't erase from where I come from. There were
many times that I wanted to be from somewhere else –
somewhere less country. Somewhere less me. Truth is, I
didn't know a lot about life outside of a small town with
close proximity by the border, until I left. When I first
went off to college in Austin,  I just nodded when someone
said things that were unfamiliar to me, until one day I didn't.

 I was about 18 and someone said they wanted to have
chips and "kay-so." And I asked "what is kay-so?" They
said, "You're Mexican and you don't know?" First of all, I
had never been called "Mexican" before. Almost everyone
in my small town looked like me, so we were just *gente*.
Perhaps we called each other Mexican American and I
liked the word Chicana – but the way they said "Mexican"
was as if it was a bad word.

I ignored the condescending tone and went with *esta gente*
to eat their so-called "kay-so." They lived in my dorm and
I was new. I wanted to make friends or was curious at the
very least. I was the only Latina person and there was one
African American man. The rest were Anglo. So we're at
the Tex-Mex restaurant and when the waiter comes to the
table, piden "chips y kay-so". I literally did not know what
they meant.

So when they brought the "kay-so" out with the salsa and
the chips, I was like "oh, that's what you meant. Queso.
As in cheese? You all were talking about melted cheese.
You call that kay-so? No wonder I didn't understand you.

I had never heard it pronounced like that. I'm guessing you don't speak Spanish, right?" I said unapologetically.

No one said anything. *Se quedaron callados* for like two seconds and then changed the subject. We ate the chips and their "kay-so" but it was so bland, *no me gusta para nada.* I had never heard Spanish butchered like that. Where I come from, we said it how it was meant to be said, or at the very least made the effort. Even non-Latinx people made the effort. It was respect for a language.

I used to get discouraged when non people of color people called out my pronunciation in English or Spanish (if it didn't fit up to their standards). I didn't understand. I rarely called them out when they mispronounced words in Spanish, unless they butchered it so badly that I didn't understand what they were saying.

I remember that one time a judge at a high school poetry competition wrote on a critique sheet to not confuse my "ch" with my "sh" sound. I swear I did not know what that lady was talking about until years later.
I'm tired of non people of color people butchering Spanish language so badly and then expecting me to pronounce English perfectly. My tongue doesn't work that way. Pinche double standard. My tongue is going to do *lo que le dé la gana.* I'm going to switch up my ch's and my sh's, *si yo quiero.* And when you call me out, I'm going to say that "I don't apologize for my tongue." *A ver que dicen.*

I can't undo what I know, where I come from, my early childhood years, or bilingual education that laid the foundation for how I pronounce words. Why does my pronunciation offend you? Yours offends me. Or your disregard for even trying. I'm frustrated that I'm having to explain myself. Even writing this frustrates me. I shouldn't even acknowledge it.

I'm writing this to tell you:
I am not apologizing for my tongue
I am not apologizing for my tongue
I am not apologizing for my tongue and
I'm going to let it do what it's gonna do.
I can't change my tongue, nor do I want to. This I know to be true.

# Chongo Story

I should have known I wasn't going to make this dance team. It was my first year in college. I always thought I was a good dancer. I had been a cheerleader for years and I was a self-taught hip hop dancer, having learned how to dance from the Janet Jackson videos I had recorded from MTV onto VHS tapes, and all the Selena concerts I had attended as a teen. Yes, THAT Selena. I mean what could be better than learning from la Janet y la Selena?
I walked in the room. I looked like none of the chicas, with their light skin and neutral colors, and me in my hot pink leggings, purple sports bra, big chongo to the side, and red lipstick. Y tambien los hoop earrings.  I felt like an exotic animal in a very ordinary place. I wanted to walk out the door as soon as I entered, but went through with the audition because I never was a quitter. I took a deep breath and with all my courage, I did my best to learn the routines. I had no classical training. I had never done any modern dance or any lyrical type of dance. *Dios mio.*
 Me and the other Latinx chica struggled through the process, but we did it. It was brutal, y'all. I mean, esas gringas laughed at me when I almost ran into a wall in my best effort to do their pinche classical bs. Me and the other chica (from Houston, I believe) just looked at each other without saying anything. We were each other's strength and we were not going to quit. Unspoken solidarity. Even if we got to the finish line, bloody and bruised -- or how they say "de panzazo."
My training had been limited, growing up in a rural small town with no dance teachers. I was my own dance teacher. Needless to say, I didn't make this team. So, I created my own space to dance, to create art y me olvidé de aquellas

elitist viejas who laughed at me. Me and my new friend parted ways and never spoke to each other ever. We just kind of gave each other an oral nod to acknowledge – as if we were saying "I see you."  Ay te watcho

Pero es verdad lo que dicen, it's empowering to see someone that looks like you, and that there is power in numbers. Gracias, amiga. We didn't win this time, pero no nos rajamos.

# Sra Petrita

Grandma,
I remember that day when the bus
from the little migrant school came to pick me
up as I looked out the front door window with the broken
mesh and you told me to be brave as I wanted to cry
you will make new friends, you said
*vas a conocer a nuevas amiguitas*, you said
I was four-years-old
you gave me my lunch in my blue Holly Hobbie lunchbox
you fixed my hair real pretty in chongitos and I cried a little as you
tugged on the knots on my hair
as I stepped on the bus you gave me a record to give to the
Teacher
if the teacher played the songs, you knew it would make me feel
better because I loved to dance
I loved standing on my toes, pretending to be a ballerina
except my songs were sung in Spanish and had lots of guitars
and trumpets
El Jarabe Tapatio, La Raspa -- traditional songs that made my heart
happy

That day was one of the happiest days of my life, abuelita
Because you made this little girl feel like she was somebody
My grandma, who gives her life to everyone
I never lacked anything because of you, abuelita
You always found a way -- saving and sewing
When you went up north to work in the fields with grandpa,
you always
Came back with brand new clothes and shoes for me
And it felt like my birthday
I wore them on the same day.

Memories of countless sweet, dulce things you've done for me
'Cuz I was a full-figured little girl (always developing faster than
I wanted)
I remember the time of how disappointed I was because
they didn't have a Girl Scout dress in my size
So you made me a Girl Scout costume just by looking at a picture
In the magazine just so I could be
In the Cinco de Mayo parade with the other Niñas
And my mom got mad at me that day when she found me eating
Piña and chile and dancing to cumbias at the plazita, because I
had wandered off
Abuelita, who to this day never gives up hope
Abuelita who senses when I'm having a bad day and will call to
see
if I'm ok
Abuelita who was born in the U.S. but only speaks Spanish and
broken
English to me

and says cute things like "lippystick" for lipstick or
"you likey?" to ask if I like something
Abuelita, sometimes I just want to fall into your arms and cry
and I know I have inherited some of your gifts that I'm just now
beginning to
understand
you have the ability to use your hands and words to heal those
you
love
like when you were doing a «limpia», a cleansing of my spirit
Because the moment I walked through your door, you could
sense that
my spirit was heavy
and you wanted to lift whatever was holding me down

You brought me immense peace afterwards
Sometimes I feel so guilty for living so far away and for not
visiting
enough
but when I call you, you say it doesn't matter because you say:
*nunca lejos de corazon,*
that I'm never far from your heart
My grandma who hugs strangers and tells people she loves them
so openly
My grandma who visits the nursing home because she feels sorry
for the elderly that don't have relatives to visit them
Grandma, you are in your 90s and I don't think you see yourself
as elderly
My grandma who will feed anyone who is hungry
My grandma who forgives and has done prison
ministry
My grandma who fears nothing, except God
a sturdy woman
Who raised 4 children and had a husband
Who worked in the fields picking sugar beets in Minnesota
Who knew work in the house and in the fields
Who sent her four children to college
Who still dreams....
And I inherited her dreams...
And someday I know that I will pass on those same dreams to a
grandchild
And they will call me grandma/abuelita.

# Xingona Prologue

Para la Hannah, la Lupe, Jory, Susana, la Britney,
Tina, Edyka, la Alex, Natalia, Mayra, Amy Z, la Nikki,
Alexandria Ocasio-Cortez y todas como ustedes
QUIÉN SE CREEN?
Who told y'all you could be so chingonas?
ALL OF Y'ALL
*Pero bueno*
It's not too late for me
*Como dice la canción, "no hay que llegar primero, pero hay que
saber llegar."*
You know how many years it took me to realize that it was
ok to be a Chingona?
To not feel guilty for being a disobedient, non-traditional,
woman
For feeling guilty for not completely being the "marrying"
kind
I mean, tradition is so deeply embedded in us, like DNA
*Pero la verdad es que yo soy una mujer desobediente,
independiente, pero a la vez cariñosa y madre*
I decided that I could be all of those things and be a
chingona
That I didn't have to start a sentence with "Excuse me, I'm
sorry to bother you, but..." a sentence passed on to me
I'm not sure where that started, but that apologetic
tradition ends with me.
I'm breaking the cycle -- today.
I come from a long line of apologetic women, strong in
their own right, who didn't cry tears and held it in, no
matter the severity of the circumstances.
But I can't be this way any longer, *porque soy gritona,
chillona, y a veces cabrona* -- but does that make me less of a

Chingona?
 You see, I've always had it in me to be Chingona
But for some reason I had this idea that I had to wait, like I
had to earn the right to be this way.
I wish someone would have told me 20 years ago that I
didn't have to wait until my fourth decade of life to be
who I really was -- *gritona, chillona, a veces cabrona -- pero a
la vez, chingona.*
 *Gritona, chillona, y a veces cabrona* – let this be my anthem
and sometimes my battle cry
I wish I would have been like these young ladies now in
their 20s who already know their power,
 who already know their strength,
 who already know que their words tienen valor –
*y que juntas podrán hacer cambios, no sólo en sí mismas pero en
sus comunidades, y en el mundo entero!*
*Estas palabras se las dedico a ustedes, you young chicas, las
meras meras chingonas* who inspire me -- who give me hope
Keep sharing, keep creating
and this cycle of silence
of asking for permission
of apologizing for things we didn't do
this cycle of shame for wanting things
has ended with you--
A generation of Chingonas. Órale.

# Articulate

For all the times I've been called articulate
Thinking it was a compliment
And Priscilla, "She's so articulate" he said on the llamada
Immediately una colega sent me a message and said "as if
you're NOT supposed to be articulate."
You're articulate, said the white privileged man to the
older brown woman.
He might as well have said "Oh wow, and you speak
English so well too."
It wouldn't be the first time I would hear those things
Mira, vato. I don't need you to call me articulate
I AM fucking articulate
Your tongue can't even pronounce all the words I can
pronounce without someone having to really listen hard
to interpret what you said
I'm like "Mira. how am I supposed to fucker. How am
I supposed to know what you say when you sound
like your words were just spun through a blender" y a ver
que sale
My tongue is sharper than yours. How many languages
can you actually speak?
And don't come at me with that pretexto that you took
that you took French or German in high school instead of
Spanish
It's like you all get together and decide the kind of
responses you tell multi-lingual brown people
What kind of pendejada is that
It's like you think you're smarter - -and you only speak
one language
Your world is linear
No curves

Same boring flavorless language
I feel sorry for you, ese
I shouldn't even call you ese
You're certainly not one of us
Or down with the brown
You've made that quite clear
Just go back to your world and your Shakespeare or
whatever the hell you think culture is
"But I love Pablo Neruda" you say
If you want to talk to me, come back when you actually
have brown friends
Not just the people that cut your yards or clean your
houses
Oh, and you're so proud of that, thinking you are
supporting us
Do you even know their names or their families or
anything about them?
We're not your fucking hired help.
We're people.
Until you learn to humanize us, get the fuck outta here.

# Selena 1989

*Baila baila esta cumbia*

Immortal words of la reina del Tex Mex
Selena Quintanilla Perez
Presente!
Selena helped me reclaim my culture
my language
my identity
I was lost somewhere
between MTV videos
and the norteño music
that blared at church festivals
and kitchen radios
Selena was all of this --
She was la Janet Jackson
la Donna Summer
y también la Vicky Carr
 I was a brown-skinned 15-year-old girl
Who found herself in this 19-year-old singer
Mi primer concierto--
1989
in a southwest Texas dance hall
in Crystal City
the chanteuse
who did non-stop vueltas on stage
her turns were sharp and smooth
she moved across the stage with the grace of a ballerina
pero con alma de GITANA
Selena was a teenage high priestess
Who hypnotized us and
Spoke to us

So we followed
Confident
Unapologetic
My generation of brown girls and brown boys,
Had found their idol
1989 --
The year I began to wear red lipstick
Selena Red
I started learning the lyrics to her songs
in Spanish
A language I had chosen not to speak so much back then
I could relate to Selena
She too had lost her Spanish
But was reclaiming it
After Selena
I started feeling proud of my brown-ness
 and all its glory
I took down the Molly Ringwald and picture and replaced
with Selena
To the discomfort of my father,
That's when I became
A spandex-wearing
Red-lipstick wearing
Hoop wearing
Selena wannabe.

# Santos, Como eras?

*[This piece is an homage to Santos Rodriguez, a 12-year-old child, who was murdered on July 24, 1974 by Dallas Police officer Darrell Cain. This is for Santos and all the brown boys whose lives were cut short by those entrusted to protect us. Although treated as if they were adults, they simply were just boys. And I often ask myself: What was Santos the boy like? Before the brutal murder. Who was Santos, the child who lived in the Little Mexico neighborhood in Dallas? I ask: Santos, como eras?" Santos, how were you?]*


What kind of music did you listen to ?
Did you sing "bad bad Leroy brown"
When you hung out with your brother or con tus amigos
Or maybe Jim Croce wasn't your style
Did you like those Mexican rancheras de Flor Silvestre y
Antonio Aguilar that your abuelo played
Did you roll your eyes when older primos and primas
listened to "Me and Mrs Jones"
Grown ups can be so cheesy, no?
Or maybe you were more of a Deep Purple music kind of
kid, playing records of "Smoke on the Water," dreaming
of a Summer that all of us at 12-years-old dream of
What DID you dream about?
Did you want to be an astronaut? Or a teacher? Or a
lawyer? Or maybe you loved cars so much that you
dreamed of fixing them
Painting them candy apple red or a midnight blue
Or maybe you dreamt of driving to the Grand Canyon
Did you play sports or maybe you were more of an artist?
Did you like Science and looked up at the stars trying to

connect constellations and wondering what it was like to walk on the moon?

Did you catch frogs and horned toads in the backyard of your abuelo's porch and play street ball like so many of us did back then?

Santos, I think we would have been friends. I bet you were the coolest kid, so cool that everyone in Little Mexico liked you.

When you would walk down the street decian, "Hey, ay viene el Santos"

El Santos --

That must have been so cool to have a name like Santos – it reminds of the great luchador "El Santo"

In fact, you are kind of like our Santo

Most of our names are forgotten after we're gone, but yours Santos, it lives on and on.

In fact, your name is so dope that there's a park named after you aqui- y en Washington state.

How many kids can say that?

But you know what, Santos?

I wish there weren't parks named after you?

I wish we didn't have to shout your name in the streets so people could remember your name.

And all the names of brown boys taken by police officers No, murdered.

I wish you were out there shouting with us, Presente!

I wish you and I were friends and that we could visit your old neighborhood in Little Mexico and say "mira nomas. I remember when…."

Ay Santos, I bet you have some funny stories, and some sad ones too.

Some really sad ones

Too sad for any 12-year-old or for any adult

Santos, Santos, you are as presente as ever
*No te olvidaremos*
*Esos curls que tenias en tu cabello, esa sonrisa de niño bueno*
*una fotografía eternamente grabada en nuestros corazones,*
*y en redes de internet*
*Ay tu mama*
*Como estará?*
I think of her all the time
And I think of you too, Santos

# Love Letter To My Children's Future Children, Great Grandchildren And Future Generations

*[Inspired by Da Grove cohort workshop session facilitated by Sharon Day and Virginia Grise]*

**For Pleasant Grove**

A song: *Es tan importante saber que yo te amo*
A letter: I am sending love to all my future great grand-
children,
and even several generations forward
To all of our great grandchildren,
 grand nieces,
grand nephews,
and all the future children of nuestra comunidad
de aquí de Pleasant Grove
My radical dream for you is that from the day you are
born
you know that you are loved
That the prayers and love of everyone in your family and
community
 protect you desde el momento que nazcas
That the seeds we plant today
 bring you beautiful gardens to play in,
to dream in,
to feel safe in
I want you to know that your tatarabuela loves you
immensely

and sends all her love forward
I want you to know this
And receive this
Tu bisabuela o tatarabuela
Wherever I am in your lineage
 es una loca
una loca soñadora
que quiere crear nuevos mundos solo para ti
I want you to know that your great grandma or great great
grandma
 is a crazy lady
a crazy dreamer that wants to create new worlds for you
Te amo
Con todo mi corazón
even if I might never have the chance to hold you in her
arms
No importa
Mi amor para ti siempre estará presente
Long after I'm gone
My dream for you is for you to live your biggest,
 most beautiful dream
That you carry the courage of all of your past abuelas
and all the ancestors who walked before you
El amor de tu gente
That loves you
Echale ganas mijas y mijos
You are beautiful and loved
Beautiful and loved
Beautiful and loved
May your gardens be abundant and beautiful

# Jose Canseco

Broadcast Journalism sequence. Fall 1994. UT Austin.
Students laugh when I'm the sports anchor in a student
newscast and I say the name JOSE CANSECO, with
apparently an accent- an accent I didn't know I had. My
classmates laugh. I want to cry or punch them in the face –
or both.

Three white girls are cast as the main news anchors in
our student newscast the following week. The other three
Latinas in the class and me I look at each other when the
guys mention how the three Anglo girls "are the best
looking anchors we've had." I imagined what we all
thought. It wasn't just this, it was so many things. This
seemed insignificant compared to the other things that
had been happening. The persistent racism. There were no
other persons of color in the class besides us.

I was from a small town that no one had ever heard about.
The white classmates didn't even remember my name.
They confused me and the other three Latinas all the time.
We were nameless. We were simply the "brown girls"
or the "Selena girls." For the first time in my life, I felt
unpretty, insignificant

THEY were going to learn my name before the semester
was over. Priscilla, Itza, Elizabeth and Stephanie were
not just going to be the SELENA (interns), but we were
going to have a fucking name. Yes, some said we actually
looked like Selena. We all look alike, right? The four of us
joined forces and took our fight to the dean of the College
of Communications. The four of us stood in solidarity as
we voiced our concerns to the student body and dean over
what was happening - as if they didn't know already.
The most passionate of our group was Elizabeth. To this

day, she's one of my heroes. There's a bond that I will forever feel with these ladies for the rest of my life. "You made us feel like lepers!" una amiga told them, as I stood there with watery eyes. She TOLD them. Some of them cried or acted offended and called themselves victims – white tears at its very best. We were gaslit and ostracized by some. But others came up to us and simply said "I'm sorry."

I think I have blocked most of the events that took place at the College of Communications meeting that day with the dean of students. I thought it was interesting how the following semester the university made it a requirement for ALL communications students to take some type of diversity class. It simply wasn't enough. But it was a start. We passed on the baton to the next. And we still continue the fight, wherever we are…

# Homegirl poem.

I'm still that home girl from Crystal City
Who lived on Highland Circle
Who wears chola red lipstick and hoop earrings
Who still jams to Selena and Little Joe
And whose border Spanglish pronunciation bleeds into
her vowels, even when she speaks "proper" English
That's me.
I talk to everyone as if they were old friends and I open
doors for the elderly and children, because it's the right
thing to do
That's the way I was raised
If I don't have anything good to say about someone, I
don't say it at all because I save my fire for when it really
counts.
I don't speak venom.
I speak praise.
Because our people have suffered and we all suffer.
Healing must commence somehow.
From within.
This is my own homegirl code.
I've borrowed philosophies from abuelas and uncles and
wise people I've met on the street.
I collect memories and stories in my brain and in
notebooks I keep in every corner of my existence
If I'm your friend, I'll be loyal to you until the end.
And if you truly know me, you know all of the above to be
true.

# Ay Nena Nena

I like the way my body looks in the shadows
It's silhouette (*tan curvy la nena*)
Or *como se ve*
On a Sunny Day
walking on the sidewalk con tacones
pa pa pa pa - con mis caderas moving from side to side

Or the other day when I caught a glimpse of it as I was
walking down the stairs in a parking garage
*Ay Nena Nena*

I said
You are even naughtier in shadows
Your waist looks smaller
And those hips exaggerated
And you look taller too
And we won't even want to talk about that bumbum

*Ay Nena Nena*
Is this your interpretation of me?
Is this how you see me?
Dear shadow
I'm giving you a name
From now on, your name is Ay Nena Nena
Just like that

Maybe you're the better version of me
If I wasn't you and you weren't me, I'd be crushing on you too.
Orale. Que self- esteem, no?

Todos los demas can take their «other» standards

elsewhere
*Que se vayan pa'l carajo*
*Ay Nena Nena*

Even when physical me thought her body wasn't adequate
One look at you, and I thought damn' who is this sexy bitch
I want to know her, I want to be her
Every day I aim to be you
*Ay nena nena*

My alter ego
The bigger, more beautiful,
 more sexy,
 film noire
Jessica Rabbit
version of me
When you look extra chula I call you 'Ay Nena Nena'
That's what the Argentino used to say to me
He must have caught a glance of you too, Nena
*Ay Nena Nena*

You show up at the right times
I may have been having a rough day and then you appear
Out of nowhere, in the shadows
And I say, ay nena nena, you sexy cabrona
 And then I remember that I'm you, Nena
And I know that I'm going to be fine
*Que todo va estar bien*
*Que tudo vai dar certo*
*jeitosa*
*fogosa*
*hermosa*
*Ay Nena Nena*

# Crystal City Chula/Cholx

I'm a complete mess of a woman
A broken stained-glass window
of too many things
of hot, red emotions
of Southwest Texas tierra
of sweet Sun tea
Too sugary
Too fiery
Too much
Extra as f--
I find my un-pretty side the prettiest
If I like you, maybe I'll show you this side
The scars
The visible ones
and the other ones--
The ones that appear,
 when you least expect it
*cuando menos esperas*
But be patient with me amor --
Or not --
Either way I'm okay
*Tengo cumbia, ritmo y sabor*
*en mis venas*
When I walk, *bailo*
*Con estas piernas*
*Piernotas*
Legs, strong legs
from wearing too many high heels
y too much dancing
My legs are weapons
Who needs *balas* when I have THESE

*No me crees?*
Ask the drunk man I kicked out of my car
for grabbing me
*"dónde no debería"*
*Desgraciado*
My mother called me a *strong woman*
*Eres media* Annie Oakley, she said
A skirt wearing, cabronx
I'll put you under my spell, *vato loco*
*Ven conmigo –*
Come with me
Y *bailamos*
I drink my tequila, cafe y whiskey the same way
*Me gusta saborear la vida*
Squeeze all the juice that life has to offer
*Mis emociones son grandes*
I'm a woman of big emotions (and big hair)
I will burn internally and still smile
*Pero del dolor nace el arte*
Art is born from pain
There's some things that *sabila* and
Grandma's *limpias* can't heal
I'm an angel --
No, you're the devil, dice mi EX- novio
But I'm a good girl
But El diablo is also a good person, he says
whatever
Call me *diabla*
*Santa*
*Loca*
*Madre*
I'm none of those things
Or maybe, I'm all of those things
*Quién sabe*

# Braiding Roots

The Earth
The Moon
The Sun
My sons
My parents
My cousins
My uncles
My beautiful tias
And my close friends-- my chose family
Long line of sturdy mestiza women who worked the land
And braided dreams
Who planted gardens
That gave fruit to generations
And filled bellies
I pick up the Earth in one hand
And seeds in the other
And I want to spread the dirt in my hair and plant the seeds,
 so that I can someday become part of the Earth
And walk with my *ancestros* who worked the land
For my feet to disappear
And grow into the ground
And my arms to become like branches
For birds to build nests
In my trees
And the caterpillars and *mariquitas* to crawl on my nose
I want my roots to dig deep in the earth
So that I can be planted
And watch future generations grow
The transformation of a *Nigulha Tsutsu*
To a tree of the Earth
With the fruit of a *mujer sabia*.

# Frijoles con tortillitas

*Jesucita Hernandez...presente!*
Senora Chita with her long silver hair she would braid,
hanging on both sides of her head
Like columpios
With ribbons she would find here and there
And bobby pins that never matched her silver hair
Her eyes had wrinkles around them, but when she smiled,
It was as if a child was looking at you.
She wore house dresses and pantuflas
Sometimes blue with florecitas or pink with florecitas
But the purple one was my favorite
Y cada dia after school, you could smell the fresh pot of
frijoles and the corn tortillas on the comal
Sra Chita always had tortillitas fresh from the comal and
frijolitos con queso,
At my request
I liked queso with everything
I still do!
She would call my brother "papasito blanco" -- I don't
know how I remember that, but I do
And I was "la reina", as she called me
Chita loved us both the same but she and my brother had
a special bond
She had him so chiflado, mimado, and spoiled
I mean that gordito could do anything he wanted and get
away with hit
He had the face of an angelito and the character of a little
demonio
A trickster
And I the dreamer, who sat on her old fashioned 1950s
style table with the blue plastic tablecloth. The kind that

sticks to your elbows
While watching *el chavo del Ocho* and *Chepillin* on the tv
Even then, English was not my favorite language
And neither was it Chita's
I don't think she ever spoke English
Although her daughter Leti spoke to us in English


Chita would let us roll down the hill in the back of her
house
Getting thorns/espinas stuck to our blue jeans or legs --
depending on what time of year it was
She lived in the housing authority side of town
It never occurred to me that Chita was poor
She was the richest person I knew
She taught us what berries we were allowed to eat from
trees and were not poisonous
Played hide and seek with us
Had the patience to comb and braid my long, thick hair
And she had all these colors and fotografias all over the wall
If Chita wasn't rich, she sure was magic
She used to let all the neighbor kids come play with me
and my bratty brother--
La Cindy, Gerardo, Velma, el Kelly, y Adrian.
Chita fed us, nurtured us, gave us a safe place just to be
--- to be kids.
She created a magical space that I still return to in my
mind as an adult.
My grandma Petra and grandpa Luis would sometimes
stop by Chita's house to drop off hot plates of food -- some
carnita with calabacitas, or some caldo de res and arroz
-- a small offering to show gratitude for the love that Chita
showed their grandchildren
My grandparents knew that we could never repay her in

this lifetime for what she gave me and my brother
The day Chita stopped taking care of us was the hardest day of my little girl life.
My brother and I cried for days
We gave future caregivers a hard time
There was only one for us -- Dona Jesucita Hernandez with the braided silver hair
My brother and I constantly asked my mom to take us to see her.
El pobrecito de mi hermano even ran away from home, to get to her house
We found him safely of course
In front of Johnny's house, which was the day their long friendship started
My brother had ended up on Johnny's front yard, as he was trying to find his way to Chita's house
He was in elementary school
How crazy is that!
Chita never stopped loving us and we never stopped loving Chita
I can't even mention her name to my brother
In this life when we reflect of the people that truly loved us, unconditionally -- flaws and all
Dona Chita is at the top of the list

# Memoria of my girl scout dress

You told me my dress didn't come in
outta stock in my size or something like that
I stood there for a moment and you were sad for me
as tears flowed down my cheeks
cuz I wanted to be in the parade so badly
So you came up with a solution the best way you could
bought some fabric
to try to match the "Girl Scout brown" in the catalog
It was a lighter shade of brown but it didn't matter
So grandma took on the task of sewing me my own
original dress
She made the dress perfectly
without a pattern
Except the buttons
the big white kind and you thought lining the pockets
on the outside with eyelet lace would be a nice feminine
touch.
the finished product--
a light brown girl scout Brownie uniform
an original Petra Ramos creation with love
the uniform looked almost identical to the Brownie
uniform in the catalog
except mine looked more girly
the day of the parade my mom brushed my long, black
curly hair that covered my back
and I cried a little as she tried to gently tug away at the
tangles
In a short time, my hair was in full, long pigtails
with my light brown dress with the big white buttons
I wore those socks that almost came up to my knees (Girl
Scout brown, of course)

and my shoes were polished
such love and care to make a little 2nd grader happy
little girl so insignificant to the WORLD but to a mother
and grandmother, she was the WORLD…
So I reached into my pocket y me puse una sonrisa
and mom drove me to the parade.

# Home

Home is the place where my Grandma Petra lets me take a nap
And I wake up to the sounds of Cornelio Reyna and Ramon
Ayala music playing on an old kitchen radio
And there's always warm tortillas (fresh from the comal) and
fideo to eat in the afternoon
Home is where my tias Irma, Olga, mom Rosa and prima
Roseana laugh in the kitchen and share stories
"I remember when..." Or "remember that time when we had the
ugliest dolls?"
Home is Leo's and Cristiano's smile
It's the sound of my mom's and dad's voice saying "mija"
Home is dancing cumbias for the first time with my Grandma
Lorena, my first dance teacher
Home is the place where i saw my brother play baseball at Juan
Garcia Park
Where spectator kids would run to catch foul balls and turn
them in to the concession stand for a free raspa/snow cone.
Home is the place where i went bike riding with my grandpa
Oscar
Where i worked at the family store during the summers
Home is watching my grandpa Luis' fat cat Frank with the big
blue eyes, get lost in the front yard plantitas
Home is going to the tiendita (the corner store) with grandpa
Luis to pick up his Sunday newspaper
Home is the place where my friends call me Prissy
Where no one gets old
Where grandpas and neighbors and cousins never die
And the boys and girls of Summer throw water balloons at each
other.

# Critic Review/Afterword:

I just finished reading the new book by Lopa Banerjee and Priscilla Rice titled 'WE ARE WHAT WE ARE: *PRIMAL SONGS OF ETHNICITY, GENDER & IDENTITY'.*

It is in two parts and prefaced by a short introduction by Dr. Santosh Bakaya. The first part is by Lopa Banerjee. I have been reading her work right from her first memoir/narrative nonfiction 'Thwarted Escape' (2016) and this book showcases her development, one I am proud to recognize and record, as being a powerful, intense writer who seemed to always have an ability to write in imagery that left one a bit stunned, rich in the five senses. But here she has developed also in terms of themes and range which was what I felt was lacking in the earlier work without losing out on her power, imagery, sensuousness and intensity.

She has written nonfiction/memoir, poetry, fiction, been an editor for anthologies, done interviews, written criticism and reviews, as well as essays, and been a translator and teacher and the result is that finally her poems are not only vehicles of art but also education. They look at the West both critically and appreciatively, with a post-colonial and diaspora bound stance naturally. Lopa living in USA, is a feminist and her identification is not only with Kamala Surayya, and Taslima Nasrin, but also with Frida Kahlo, Simone de Beauvoir and others that show that there is not just a questioning but also a bridge. The most striking thing here is the width of her themes which is such that if some are alienated by some poems being too predictably Bengali or Indian, some others will be drawn precisely to those poems for the very same reasons, and this two-edged sword which is the nature of her poems compels me to admire her. To be honest, it is difficult to nitpick or find fault with Lopa's poems in this collection as in poem after poem we find lines we can echo, are dazzled by and relate with. She writes on her mother, her family, her grandmother, her love for Kolkata, Durga, Bengali artists and art she admires, the Kaal Baisakhi, Indian slokas and scriptures, death, herself, love, sex, romance and a hundred other things with an unashamed abandon that it is hard not to get carried away by. The range of emotions is no longer that of a person who is bound by melancholy but richer exploring all the dark emotions and colors with a vengeance. In the poem 'I Exist', she refers back to Maya Angelou, Sylvia Plath and Mahasweta Devi as other influences on her, all of them worthwhile ones like Virginia Woolf, and ends by saying with a characteristic note of humility:

"I exist, a minuscule, shameless revolution
Floating in a tiny, raging bottle of wants."

My point or bone of contention would probably be that with this set of poems I am no longer so sure that Lopa is either miniscule or tiny as a poet. She is rather huge and Amazonian. Indian literature is full of people who make anthologies and say this is the present world of Indian literature or contemporary literature. While I do not know if Lopa appears in them or not, her poems testify to me that here is a voice that very much represents much of not only what is worth reading in present day Indian English writing or writing in English from West Bengal and Kolkata and in post-colonial discourse as well as in diaspora related literature but also as feminist literature of Indian and global relevance.

I must admit to the curiously contradictory fact that while

Lopa herself decries the male gaze that wants to reduce women to body or bodies, her lines on sexuality and sensuality attract me with their vigor and multifaceted layers, as if they breathe with a life of their own, "inviting and inciting" me.

Thus, in this book of prose, drawings, paintings and poems, lines like this beckon me and tantalize me:

"In the month of Virgo, my femaleness aches,
I free it from my moist breasts, from my deliriously happy arms,
From my rivulets of tears. I let it roam, threadbare.
*Yatra naryetsu pujyante ramante tatra devata…*"
They say: Gods rejoice within my pleats and folds,
I become the tender quiet of the beautifully stoic *Yogini*,
I become the pomegranate blood-drops of my majestic *Kundalini*."

Reading them my maleness aches, and they are a powerful testimony to the ability of poetry to invoke not only *Stree* or *Nari shakti* but also the *Ardha Nareeshwara* and the yin and yang. I could go on about this set of poems by her but will leave the rest to the reader to wrestle with. In the end, I want to say that Lopa needs to be studied, keeping in mind writers like Staurt Hall and Homi Bhabha and many others she herself quotes or does not, writers like Ananis Nin, but however she is studied, whether contextually or just by reading only her, the effort leaves one richer and in love with the texture of her poetry, its depths, volcanoes and fiery outbursts as well as it tears, moans and complaints and its multiple splendid suns and moons or darkness.

Lopa's themes and subjects here are so wide that I could keep extending this note and all of them deserve attention and are worthy of being talked of. She had come of age or arrived finally, with a bang and not a whimper, here in themes and subjects too, including Buddha, workers who suffered and so many other images like America, the Ganges and Kumartuli. not to mention how to be a badass (woman?) poet.

Priscilla Rice reminds me, at a tangent of another of my favourite writers, presently, who is Elizabeth Marino. To talk of her from the point of view of identity politics is a scary prospect simply because I want to talk of her the way she wants me to. I want to recognize all of her identities and simply let her be, to summarize her first essay, and even saying this this way sounds somehow presumptuous for which I feel apologetic. But to come to the poems.

The mesquite tree haunts us as do her ancestors who worked the land. What strikes us immediately is the honesty of Rice's poetry. Simple and direct with no attempt to varnish it except with what it is already decorated, by proper Spanish which leads to her kind of patois. The mix of her language which seems to me English and Spanish but to her may be Spanish first and then English at times, is just enchanting to my ears when I try to read it aloud and try to understand the half of it which I don't, much, as are her characters. These are characters I have met from the other side, from the eyes of white 'men' and writers like Greene and Steinbeck but to meet them from the inside is a totally different experience as in the poems of a Marino or a Rice. I feel not only enlightened but ennobled, as in Lopa's poems, when Rice speaks of her grandmother and mother and trees. I feel at home when she speaks of being bilingual, something I to know of, and of her love for dance, being self-taught, and not being a quitter and going about it her own way. I feel a fierce sense of kinship. Her "Abuelita", and her desire to be one in the future, remains with me. We go through the poems written by Priscilla and Lopa and certain common themes emerge, which include the discrimination against skin color, against being from a different place, in both "home" and "abroad", but poverty and class differences as well as growing up in a rural surrounding throw their shadows on Rice's work a bit more, as backgrounds that help us appreciate the struggle to come out of them, and the necessity for education and faith to do so. The feminist note is also similar, where Rice admires her mother and ancestors for being strong women, despite being apologetic women, but says she has come to break the tradition, not being the marrying kind and that she has also admiration for the younger generation who bring in continuity by rupture.

"Keep sharing, keep creating
and this cycle of silence
of asking for permission
of apologizing for things we didn't do
this cycle of shame for wanting things
has ended with you--
A generation of Chingonas. Órale."

A fine evocation of the right kind of rebellion can be found in these lines. Her ode to Selena Red and her "get the fuck outta here" are similarly stirring when said to the one who tells her she is "articulate." She identifies with the earth, with her sisters who are Latinas, with her people whom she introduces us to, with Jessica Rabbit, and in her poems on what it means to be a woman and on wanting to be one with the earth, she identifies with Lopa; there is a similarity that one cannot escape. There is a sincerity and a gaiety and a reaching out for healing one can't escape, either, and does not want to, despite the racism faced and the discrimination, and because of the awareness of the need for activism, reaching out for life and freedom and the self-realization that she finally has, in these poems and her art, ACHIEVED.

*Dr. AV Koshy*
*Acclaimed author, poet (Pushcart Nominee), short story writer, critic, researcher and academician, editor and anthology maker who has started the Reuel International Prize for Literature, runs an NPO on autism, invented the Roseate Sonnet form and founded the Significant League with Reena Prasad. He has 25 books to his credit with his name on the cover. He is presently a Visiting Professor in Jain University.*

## Black Eagle Books

www.blackeaglebooks.org
info@blackeaglebooks.org

Black Eagle Books, an independent publisher, was founded
as a nonprofit organization in April, 2019. It is our mission
to connect and engage the Indian diaspora and the world at
large with the best of works of world literature published on
a collaborative platform, with special emphasis on
foregrounding Contemporary Classics and New Writing.

Lightning Source UK Ltd.
Milton Keynes UK
UKHW010730010822
406672UK00002B/383